Positioned to Birth MORE!

DISCOVER THE GIFT OF GOD IN YOU

By: Nadia Olivia Clyne

~DEDICATION~

This book is dedicated back to the

Author & Finisher of my Faith!

The Lord of my life, The Alpha & The Omega

My Commander, My Healer, My Advocate,

My CEO- Jesus Christ.

Thank you for stretching me and challenging me

to be MORE!

~TABLE OF CONTENTS~

Phase 4: Delivery

Phase 5: RECOVERY

~ACKNOWLEDGEMENTS~

To Solé and Sevyn… You are beautiful and amazing. You both are the best pieces of me. You have taught me that the best of me is yet to come. You love me unconditionally and you teach me daily. Through you I have learned patience and unconditional love. Because of you, I am.

To my husband, Nicholas... Thank you for believing in me when you didn't see. I thank God for allowing our paths to cross and allowing us to do this journey of life together.

To my parents, Ferdinand & Berthelia... Thank You for being the best teachers of life that I could ever have in human form. I am built the way I am because of the foundation you gave me and for that I will forever be grateful. Thank you for loving me and pushing me to be my best in everything I did.

To my Pastor, Dr. Chermain Lashley... Thank you for seeing me. You have been a wonderful teacher, mentor and friend. You showed me that I am never alone, that the Holy Spirit is always with me. Your wisdom, impartation, leadership and covering has blessed my life and all those attached to me tremendously.

To my sisters, Ianthe & Anika... In our differences there is a bond that can't be broken. Thank you for loving me at all stages of me and for always being my biggest fans.

To my Sisters in Christ, my "Elizabeths"... Thank you for pushing me, believing in me and helping me to deliver when I thought I couldn't.

To my Treasured Army, thank you for always being there when needed. Your loyalty is unmatched and I will be forever grateful for your willingness to serve.

To my cousins, no matter near or far, thank you for allowing me to teach you and for teaching me through our many endeavors.

To my "Heavenly Holy Ghost Filled Hitters", Dr. Rev. Charmain Lashley, Bishop Jacqueline McCullough, Pastor Annette Cutino, Apostle Rose Stewart, and Pastor Ebony Small. I thank God everyday for you. You have helped me to grow into the woman God has called me to be when I couldn't see. I am forever grateful for your obedience to Him.

Lastly, thank you to everyone who ever prayed with me and for me. Thank you for allowing me to trust God in me through this entire birthing process…

It's just the beginning… I Love All of You!

~A SPECIAL INVITATION FROM NADIA~

This book was not written to just tell a story but rather to build faith based relationships and connections with like minded women from all around the world who have a desire for more. It is for women who wake up on purpose, filled with intention to allow God's glory to shine through them no matter the circumstance. I am speaking to women who are ready to give birth or have already given birth to the unlimited possibilities of the purpose that is within all of us while helping others do the same.

As the founder and creative strategist of the Treasured Empire, a faith based lifestyle brand that includes The Treasured Beauty Hair Lounge, Treasured Beauty Skincare and Treasured Hands, a creative development program for women and children, I feel that I have a responsibility to create an online community where clients can come together to connect, get encouragement, share treasured life hacks and, support one another through prayer. This is why this book was written and my hope is that it can become one of the most positive, engaging, and supportive online communities in the world. A place where women from all around the world can live a life without compromising who they are meant to be. This online community is a place where faith, beauty and creativity can live harmoniously.

If you don't mind, help me reach my goal of connecting with women from around the world by just going to www.iamnadiaolivia.com and request to join The Treasured Circle with Nadia on Facebook. There you will immediately connect to myself and a group of women who have a desire for more, women who are already living a Treasured Life, and some who started but don't know how to do and be more. Allow this group to be a transparency tool to help you live in an abundance of advice, guidance, and support to help you live a life of greatness.

I'll be moderating the community and checking in regularly, so I look forward to seeing you there! If you would like to reach out to me personally on social media, follow @IamNadiaOlivia on Facebook and @Iamnadiaolovia on Instagram. Let's connect soon!

~Forward~

BY REV. DR. CHERMAIN LASHLEY

Feelings of weakness and vulnerability; hopelessness and despair; often become the place of stagnation for many of us. The emotional brokenness we encounter, even as Christian believers, have caused so many to miss the message that we are God's vessels and that we have God's treasures in us. As a result, many of us have lived clueless to our kingdom assignment and purpose. The manifestation of purpose begins with knowing who and whose we are.

The Bible tells us *"But we have this treasure in earthen vessels, that the excellence of the power may be of God and not us" ...always carrying about in the body the dying of the Lord Jesus that the life of Jesus also may manifest in our body." (King James Bible, 2 Corinthians 4:7, 10)*

What is this treasure that the apostle Paul writes to the church about? This is the treasure that is inside of every born-again believer. This treasure is the death and resurrection of Jesus our Savior and Lord. The death of Jesus speaks of self-denial, which means resisting the temptation to rely solely on self and our human abilities independent of Christ. It is an inability to trust the Lord to help us in those difficult moments that hinders the working of the Holy Spirit to bring into our prophetic destiny. In our flesh we incline to fix our wounds using various methods, avoidance, sometimes we cover up; medicate; act out and the list goes on. But whenever these methods are used, we eventually become imprisoned in a life of survival mode, where we are left to merely exist without truly living.

The first death Jesus died happened in the Garden of Gethsemane when he surrendered the will of his flesh to the Father's will. *"Oh My Father if this cup cannot pass away from Me, unless I drink it, your will be done." Matthew 26:42.* This is the death we must carry if we are going to birth God's purpose for our lives.

How is death a treasure? Jesus rose up after he died. The resurrection power of Jesus is also God's treasure working new life in us. New birth becomes inevitable, because while His death is working, His resurrection life is also working in us. In Him we have power to rise up from every stormy situation, trials; unfair treatment, so that we can give birth to His will for our lives. The same Holy Spirit that raised Jesus, uses the difficult experiences to prepare and empower us to give birth to more than we can see. The Spirit is always willing to lead the way but we must take our flesh out of the driver's seat and let him lead us.

The author of these pages, Nadia Olivia Clyne, has been inspired by the Holy Spirit to raise awareness of Godly purpose and to point us to the spiritual birthing process that will help us to passionately embrace new life. In the pages of "Position to Birth More" Nadia presents an honest, straightforward discourse that will show the reader how God causes all things to work together for our good and His glory. Using Scriptural foundation; and symbolism of natural pregnancy as well as intimate moments of her life and her life-changing testimonies, Nadia beckons us into our Godly greatness. She also provides support through coaching; nurturing as well supplying mentoring and networking opportunities where needed.

Her "keeping it real" approach will help the readers to journey from pain to purpose, enabling them to see evidence of how the Holy Spirit empowers us to use negative experiences; designed to rob us, to give birth to greater. Every person reading this book will come to understand that God has treasured us with all we need to birth more than we can imagine.

Have you started the journey to fulfilling your God given assignment? Are you engaged in doing work that you are called to do; work you want to do; or are you just doing? There is a difference between working to survive and receiving fulfillment while working. This book will give you the tools that can assist you in addressing these questions and help you position your mind for all that is in store for you. I challenge you to read and explore the wisdom of these pages and gain a better understanding of what it means to prepare yourself for greater.

-Dr. Rev. Chermain Lashley,

Senior Pastor

Grace United Methodist Church

CAN YOU SEE ME?

A rhetorical question I often asked myself throughout my life was, "Can you see me?" I often felt invisible in a visible world. Living day to day in a world where I was defined by what I looked like, the designers I wore, and who I knew. I struggled to find myself because although I thought I knew who I was, I was actually being tormented day in and day out by who I really was. The real me was fighting to come out. Being confined to a definition of myself that was expected of me made me feel like I was in a headlock. Many of us think and say we are independent and free to be who we truly are but the truth is we are really not. We are actually defined by what those around us think and expect of us. I used to sleep and dream of freedom in a way I could never explain and waking up to my reality was painful. Somehow I knew that "this" was not my normal, I knew there was more. I knew I was destined to be and do more with my life, my reality at the time just didn't align with my visions. But with hope, I knew I would become who I was destined to be. Along the way I developed some things like faith, creativity, intention and identity that helped me to become the best version of myself and birth my purpose.

I grew up as a young girl who felt lost, confused and desperate. I never thought that I would one day become a confident woman of God, who possesses unlimited possibilities of His glory. You see what you see today is not who I was always. The trials and tribulations of my life and how God positioned me is what got me to be the woman I am today. When I found God I was broken, hurt and bleeding with bandages only He could see. He saw me because He created me. He saw me dim my own light countless times to allow others to shine. He knew that if just given a chance, I would shine so brightly that not even darkness could cover me. If you have ever felt like this I want to encourage you and let you know there is hope and just as God found me, He will find you too.

"And I am convinced and sure of this very thing, that He who began a good work in you will continue until the day of Jesus Christ, developing [that good work] and perfecting and bringing it to full completion in you".~Philippians 1:6

God wants to birth out His purpose (what He designed you to be and do) through you as He did through me in every possible way. No matter the situation, you can give birth to your purpose because it was destined to happen from the very beginning, all you have to do is believe. Now I won't lie, it's a battle of sacrifice, submission and surrender to His will and not to your own. Please know it is possible for God to use an imperfect person to do great things.

Now I know you might be wondering, how can He see you if you can't even see yourself. I know because I felt the same way. Often times when we look at ourselves we see chaos, confusion and despair but when God looks at us, He sees a true gem waiting to be discovered. All we need is a little cleaning up. We may be a little dirty but all things that are treasured are. Even a beautiful, rare gem like a diamond is found deep inside the earth and has to be cleaned up for its true beauty to be revealed before it's treasured forever. Like the diamond, He digs deep inside of us to reveal our true selves, and treasures us for ever. He loves us and He wants to help us. He wants to give us a voice. He wants to give us what we were born for, true freedom. Not freedom to do whatever we want, but free from the bondage of sin so that we can walk in alignment with our heavenly Father, and be the person He created us to be through His grace.

But we have this treasure in earthen vessels, the excellency of the power being from God and not from ourselves
~ 2 Corinthians 4:7

Here is what I had to learn and I hope you will too… people like you and I were not born to fit in. We are different. We were born to stand out. Unfortunately, we tend to overcompensate in other areas to make up for that fact. We are gifted and talented but we need the right spirit to allow these things to help us be the great women we were destined to be. Sadly, we have equated our worth to being misunderstood and unvalued for far too long. Being someone you are not can be exhausting and I am here to tell you that you don't have to live like that. You can be unapologetically who you were meant to be and you don't have to compromise your integrity to do it. You can live a purposeful life on purpose. Would you believe me if I said that it's okay to not fit the mold that was set for you? Your purpose has already been defined and you don't need to look for it but rather listen for it. Yes, listen. Listen to your Father who created you before you were formed in your mother's womb.

I chose you before I formed you in the womb; I set you apart before you were born. I appointed you a prophet to the nations.- Jeremiah 1:5

No matter the struggles, the challenges, the betrayals, the heartbreaks and lack of opportunities, we must know that God will use it all for our good to develop us into who we were always meant to be and have the life we have always dreamt of.

A life that has purpose, meaning, and fulfillment. But here is the most important thing, in order to live that life, you have to get out of your own head. You self sabotage and make poor decisions and choices based on your pain. The truth is, you are fearful of reaching your full potential and you doubt yourself constantly because you don't think there is such a thing called "true freedom." Ask me how I know, because I was once you!

My intentions for this book are to not only bring hope by providing inspiration, empowerment and education to women of faith who struggle with seeing themselves the way God sees them but to also aid in understanding how God uses the trials and tribulations of our lives to position us to give birth to our purpose, so we can do and be M.O.R.E (Maintain, Overcome, Reposition, Experience) through his grace and mercy. I must warn you first. The content in this book is raw, unfiltered and a "NO Judgement Zone."

Journey with me as I invite you to travel with me through my spiritual birthing process so that you too can give birth as well- to your purpose that is. Bringing a baby to full term is not an easy process in the natural world as there are numerous stages and phases. In actual labor there are tools and trained people equipped with the specific knowledge who must work together to deliver a healthy baby. It is the same way in the spiritual realm when giving birth to our purpose. It was only when I received the right solution, "the treasure of God" for all of my ailments, that I was able to discover and birth my purpose.

My desire is that not only will you discover and birth your purpose but also learn and develop tools to help you live it out after reading this book. Using some of my personal testimonies, I provide tools like prayers and position principles in this book that are necessary to maintain a healthy mindset, overcome negativity such as self sabotage, doubt, depression, a poverty mindset and more so that you can reposition your mind, body and spirit in order to help reach your fullest potential. My personal goal is to unapologetically show you how to allow your pain to birth promising possibilities- Your Purpose! So that you can experience the freedom to live a life of greatness through God's grace too.

So here was my issue, I was confused as to who I was. My identity was flawed because I did not know who I was and who I belonged to. It was not until I figured where my identity was that I began to live the life I dreamt about. I went through many trials and tribulations that led to me having many spiritual abortions, some that were self inflicted. I gave up on myself multiple times from lack of identity, unworthiness and people pleasing. I also endured multiple spiritual miscarriages from lack of obedience, poor decisions and frustration. All of the emotional trauma, burnout and exhaustion left me, physically and spiritually sick. I had to have a spiritual D and C (dilation and curettage), which is a scraping of deep rooted pain from my womb from fear, disappointment, and betrayal and it was only then that I was finally able to give birth to my purpose. It didn't happen overnight but I eventually discovered that I was His treasured beauty just as He is mine. I was worthy and had value because I was made that way and God said so! Period.

Once I understood that I was able to give birth to my purpose which is to inspire, empower and educate women through beauty, faith and creativity, who like me felt unworthy. I felt at peace which is one of the feelings that let you know that you are going in the right direction. My desire is that once you understand and know the truth about who you are, whose who are, the why's and how's of how you ended up here, you can be the best of you. I pray you find healing, restoration, inspiration and comfort through my transparency and vulnerability so that you too can birth to your purpose which has infinite possibilities.

I went on an inward journey to discover who I was made to be and I found myself and my answers through the gospel of Jesus Christ. I eventually gave birth to birth my purpose, and learned to monetize my gifts and talents for His glory, in order to live my best life through wisdom, knowledge and understanding through the Word of God. I am a kingdom visionary, creator and servant and through those gifts I have become an author, speaker, entrepreneur and whatever else God wants. I could never have become any of those things without God's grace. I have also been called a Treasured Midwife, because of my gift of servanthood. Through personal development I have been trained to assist in providing healthy spiritual delivery of purpose under the leadership of Dr. Rev. Chermain Lashley.

Through my extensive journey I have learned to identify the signs of spiritual conception. By the revelation of the Holy Spirit, I can see and understand the physical discomfort and spiritual pains of a spiritual pregnancy. Allow me to help you identify these ailments and understand your journey as more than just a frustrated life through the pages of this book.

Please note, this book is not a tell-all story about my life but it serves as a testimonial tale using some parts of my life to make the points in this book real. It's about you taking time to look in the mirror and expose yourself to yourself and then bring your messiness to God so that you can have a safe delivery and birth your purpose. I take you through my entire birthing process from Conception to Recovery where you will learn about the Four Divine Phases of the Spiritual Birthing Process. Understand that this is a journey and not a destination and note delivery is just the beginning of the process. There is work to do after you discover your purpose. I wanted to make sure you have help after birth so I included, "The Intentional Plan for M.O.R.E"-4 strategic principles to help you stay in position after you discover your purpose. How to **M**aintain a healthy mindset, **O**vercome negativity, **R**eposition your mind, body and spirit in order to be able to **E**xperience true freedom through God's grace. Allow me to help you not just go through your own Spiritual Birthing Process, but learn how to achieve MORE for your life.

Journey with me because.... It's Your time to give Birth!

Phase 1: Conception

THE MINDSET

"Life Begins at Conception"

A woman giving birth to a child has pain because her time has come; but when her baby is born she forgets the anguish because of her joy that a child is born into the world.

~John 16:21

~ CHAPTER 1 ~

SEE AND SAY

But you are a chosen race, a royal priesthood, a
holy nation, a people of his own, so that you may
proclaim the virtues of the one who called you out of
darkness into his marvelous light. ~ 1 Peter 2:9

The first phase in the five phases of the birthing process is called the conception phase. The conception phase is where life begins. It is the essential blueprint for the entire birthing process. It is also known as the developmental stage. It is also the most vulnerable stage as well because this is the stage that the conditions need to be in the right order for conception to take place in order to carry your purpose/baby. The thing about this stage is that while it's the most important, it is often the stage that's the most overlooked until it's too late. For women like us who know there is MORE, this is the stage that hinders us because for us, this stage happens early in our lives. This phase is where what we see, hear, touch, taste and see sets the foundation of who we are to become and essentially determine what we birth.

This is where our identity and self image is formed. The truth is most of us were not born being told that we are made in the image of God. We were not told that we can do anything through Jesus Christ who strengthens us. We were not taught morals and values rooted in the Word of God. As our values are established they become a part of our mindset, where we begin to make choices that will affect us for the rest of our lives. Life is full of decisions, and most of us are tired of making the wrong ones. Knowing that no one is perfect, we have to realize that our decisions are based on choices, some poor and some not. Based on the things we saw during our childhood or even as adults we can sabotage this process. It's time to wake up and change our position!

> *"The only thing you sometimes have control over is perspective. You don't have control over your situation. But you have a choice about how you view it." ~Chris Pine*

~My Lights Went Out~

When I was thirteen I got slapped in my face and called a slut! It was a typical day, I was on the porch talking to my next door neighbor while I was "working out". Now, you must know I was as skinny as a toothpick but I absolutely loved being cute. On the weekends if you couldn't find me I was in the bathroom making something to put on my face, painting my toenails, putting on my mother's makeup or trying to exercise somewhere. I always knew that taking care of my body was important. I don't know if it was the cuteness of work out clothes or the colors of my mothers make up, but I just loved all things related to beauty and self-care. There was one day that sticks out in particular. I had on workout clothes- a grey sports bra and biker shorts. I was exercising on my porch and chatting to my next door neighbor. My neighbor's best friend was riding down the block & saw us outside so he stopped at the gate and the three of us were having a casual chat. One was on the ground and two of us were up on the porch. My neighbor and I sat across from each other, a healthy distance away. We chatted about going back to school and what happened over the summer. I believe school was starting back in about two weeks and so we were excited and then it happened.

My life would forever be changed after that moment. All I could see were my neighbor's friend's blank face, it was priceless. He was in as much shock as I was. I looked up and all I saw was my father's angry face as he was screaming all these hurtful words. To this day, there is a silent conversation about what happened that day.

All I remember was being called downstairs by my dad and as soon as the door opened, I was instantly slapped in the face and I fell back into the stairs and heard the word "SLUT!" I was numb. I couldn't comprehend what had just happened. Now, before you get besides yourselves let me explain. We are from the Caribbean, where emotions are not traditionally expressed as they are today. When I was growing up, "I love you" wasn't said as much but it was understood. Parents were more focused on providing for their families and they wanted their children to focus on their education and nothing else in fear that they would be taken advantage of. Yes, the ways of the older generations are different than the way they are now, but it wasn't done intentionally to hurt. Am I justifying him slapping me? No, but I am explaining that this was our way of life, our culture. To be honest, it took me a long time to understand what happened. I was so angry, mad, sad, and embarrassed. I think I felt every negative emotion there was. The only thing that kept playing over in my mind was what did I do to deserve that? What did I do? Why would he call me a slut? Why would he embarrass me like that? What was a slut, anyway? I was just talking to my friends. So now, I can't talk to boys? It was so hard for me to even think straight. All I could do was cry, I was so angry. A father was supposed to love me, tell me I was beautiful, protect me. I respected him, I looked up to him, I loved him. I was disappointed in him and myself. Didn't he know I was not "like" that.

After that day I started to look at myself differently. I never thought about my self image until that day. Now I saw myself through other people's eyes. My view of myself was distorted from an early age. Although my mother always told me that I was beautiful, to be honest it was something I didn't see. I was completely lost as to what I was getting in trouble for that day and it was that day I started to shrink. Was it because I was beautiful? Was it because I was talking to a boy or was it because I was outside? I never found out the answer because what I did realize as I got older was that it wasn't about me at all. All I remember telling myself after that day was no one would ever be able to talk to me like that EVER AGAIN! Absolutely no one would ever make me feel like that ever again. I was so confused, I never saw myself the same way again. I made a choice in that moment that I would do things my way from then on (wrong choice). Here it was, rebelliousness was creeping in. I didn't want to listen to what anyone had to tell me. Because so much chaos was going on in my home at the time I didn't tell anyone. I didn't even tell Jesus. I didn't know that I could go to God and cry it out. I did not know that I could give Him my pain. I kept it all in, I was so angry that God allowed that to happen to me that I created a wall between us. Eventually, I forgot He was there. I decided at that very moment that I had to take care of myself. That experience changed my life until I found my God given purpose.

~Distorted Views~

After that experience my view of myself and life became distorted. I knew I was no slut but the problem was, I did not know who I was. I thought I was a beautiful, smart, creative, nice girl but I started to think I was wrong. I started to question my identity because clearly I wasn't who I thought I was. Nice girls didn't get treated like that. What is a "nice girl" anyway? I remember saying to myself that since what I was doing wasn't working then I would be what "they" wanted me to be from then on. If I was going to get in trouble again it would be for something I did. Eventually I started to value what other people thought about me in every way and even tried to be perfect so that no one would have anything to say and if they did, it would be because I wanted them to. I began to change into what others wanted. I allowed their views of me to dictate who I was becoming (wrong choice #2). Looking back, I realize that incident shaped me and it wasn't what he said and it wasn't even how he said it. It shaped me because of how I allowed what he said to dictate how I began to see myself. It was not until I found Jesus later on in my life, that I saw how important it is for me to know who I was and whose I was. It did not matter how my dad saw me. It is about how I saw myself. I have learned to never let a person's view of you determine who you are.

The first thing I had to do was forgive him completely and to be honest it took a long time. But I had to realize that he is only human and said things that he did not mean but in the moment allowed his emotions to get the best of him. He was actually afraid because I was blossoming into a teenage girl and he did not know how to handle it so he handled it in the best way he knew how. Now that I am a parent I realize how hard it is to parent and how scary it is to see your children grow up in a tainted world. For me, I internalized the hurt and disappointment and it became what is called deep rooted trauma, trauma that you bury deep inside of you. Most operate out of the pain without realizing it. It went deep inside because I didn't know how to heal, it hurt so bad that words couldn't describe what I felt that day. The reality is that words hurt and it's okay to say that. I remember growing up and hearing that "sticks and stones may break my bones, but words will never hurt me." Boy, was that a lie. Words hurt, period! I know for a fact that for many years, he never knew how that day impacted me. Not talking about it led me to making numerous poor decisions after that. You may have experienced a similar situation, and it's okay. It's time to get up now and face it so you can be who you were meant to be.

Unfortunately, for my entire teenage life into early adulthood I allowed the views of others about me to shape the way I saw myself. I did not believe that I was a slut, thank God but I did start to put value on what other people said about me. It took me a long time before I realized that the most important view was how God saw me and how I saw myself. By choosing to do things my way, my view of myself and life changed. My view of myself and life became distorted. I was unable to see clearly and rebellion had settled in. I was making a lot of bad choices because of my pain and hurt that led to feelings of abandonment, rejection and disappointment which I bottled up inside of me. Because I did not know that I could've gone to my father in heaven and given it to him instead, I went looking for others to console me and the truth is that there was nothing that anyone could have said that would have made a difference. This was a battle that God and I had to face and this was just the beginning. I have found that it is more important to know who you are and whose you are, as a child of God than what you are and what you do.

~A Different Perspective~

One day in place of P.E. in eighth grade, I was introduced to Yoga & meditation. This is where I learned that I could envision myself doing and being anything that I wanted. It was the place that I first learned how to be unapologetic about what it is that I wanted for my life. We began first by laying down, getting into a comfortable position and closing our eyes. There was soft chanting music, and we began with breathing exercises and then we went into envisioning a greater version of ourselves. First, we started by acknowledging our body parts, then envisioning our environment and then ourselves; who we wanted to be, and where we wanted to be. It didn't seem bad but what it taught me was that I could do and be anything in my own power (wrong choice #3). Here is where I went wrong. I was filled with anger so I opened myself to everything opposite of what God stood for. Just as simple as that. This exercise stuck out to me because it was in that place of meditation. I wasn't being "judged" and I liked that but I also learned to rely on myself which came back to me later on. I was taught that I was the one holding all power and I was in control. At the end of the session the teacher would have us pray to other gods, which felt a bit strange but I went with it. I felt good for a little while and then when someone triggered the deep rooted pain, a load of emotions came rushing back along with another load of hurt and pain.

That was strange and so I began to ask the teacher about prayer and the god she wanted us to pray to. She wasn't happy with my questions so eventually I stopped asking and I went to my mother. She explained that there was only one true God, and it would be only through his son Jesus Christ, that I could be fully healed. That was when my love affair with God began. I wanted to know more about this God that can completely heal me. So even in the place that I should not have been, God still found me. My mother reintroduced me to prayer and I struggled for a while. I knew of prayer because I saw my grandmother and my mother do it but I didn't have a relationship with it. It was something I saw them do. I could take care of myself, I didn't need to pray and I didn't need anyone and boy was I wrong.

He wasn't close but I stood a good chance at getting to Him if I did this thing called "prayer" but it was hard. One Sunday afternoon after church I tried "meditation" at home and I decided to add prayer to the God they prayed to in church. I asked my mother to show me to pray with me and she did. She introduced me to a man named Jesus and told me that I could talk to him anytime I wanted and he would take my prayers to God. I began to speak to God through my meditations, which is now called Treasured Meditations with Jesus. I basically created a routine of things to help me to clear my mind and prepare myself to talk to God. It has developed over the years, by adding journal writing, worship, devotions and affirmations. Meditation was my first conversation with God, it helped me through my darkest days. When I was lost, unhappy, sad or confused it was there that I knew I would find my peace. I knew that there was more to this thing called life but I just didn't know what. I was able to uncover the beginning of my true self through meditation and conversations with Jesus. I knew I was destined for more. To be honest, I didn't know why all I knew was I just didn't fit in. I saw myself doing amazing things and there were times that the visions were so big they became scary. I couldn't tell anyone so I would write it. It was between my prayer meditations and writing in my journal to God that helped me get through my toughest years. I was always misunderstood and I would fight everyone because I knew that the "normal" that I was living was not my normal. If I were to be honest, I am now living out the visions I had back then. You have to 1st see where you want to be in order to get there. Dare yourself to see!"

Despite the many unwarranted trials and tribulations we must always remember that God is in it all. I know you might be saying a punch is very different from rape or molestation and I agree it is. Neither of those things should ever happen to anyone but it doesn't have to end that way. You still have the ability to envision a better ending for yourself, God already has. There are many stories in the Bible where many unfair things happen to "good" people. One story that sticks out is the story of Joseph, which I am sure you know already so I won't restate it but I will give a little perspective into it. First, Joseph's dreams were very symbolic and allowed him to envision his future.

Second, it shows that God can use trials to birth something great out in the midst of tribulation. Thirdly, if Joseph was not sold into slavery, we would never know if his family woud have been saved. Here is an account of how God used one man three times for His glory and purpose. Have you ever sat with yourself and took time to see how God is using your story for His glory?

Let's go a different direction for a moment in case you don't understand how what you view can be destructive to you birthing your purpose. Let's say you had a good childhood until you hit your 20's or 30's and now you begin looking at yourself and start to compare yourself to how many of your friends got married, who's having babies and who is next. Who has a house or two, maybe even a growing business or a booming career. Your vision becomes distorted now because you're comparing your life to someone else's. You start making good decisions based on the flawed reality you see someone else living. One of the most critical choices you will have to make in life is to decide what and who you are looking at?

I have learned that when people show you who they are the 1st time around, believe them. This was an area that I struggled with a lot and maybe you have too. I believed everyone was kind and had a "good" heart. Wrong again. I assumed everyone thought like I did and I was wrong there too. Because I didn't view myself as having any value, I attracted friends who would use me and abuse me. Here is what I did not know, for a long time I was attracting friends who suffered from the same things I suffered from like rejection and abandonment.

I didn't know all of these fancy words back then, or even the concept of them in my life but what I did know is that the raw hurtful feelings of being unwanted was too familiar. I knew I had to change something but I didn't know what. I had to do an inventory check on myself and my circle. I found myself attracting the same type of person, so I had to take a deep look in the mirror, check my symptoms and see if I was the problem. Again, you can't give birth if the conditions are not right. In the conception phase it is easy to lose what you are supposed to give birth to because you don't know what you're looking at and what you're carrying.

"Create the highest possible vision for your life,
because you become what you believe"
~Oprah Winfrey

From the age of thirteen, because my vision was distorted, I began to make choices that would send me down a slippery road. I began doing my own thing, which led to me to having multiple spiritual abortions all the way into my adut life. By trying to do life on my own I was actually repelling my purpose because that was not what I was called to do. We were never born to be in complete control of our lives. God, the one who created us, is in control. He knows the end from the beginning of our lives. He actually sees us, the real us, not the one we pretend to be but the person He shaped us to be. We just need to give Him time to complete His good work in us.

> *For I know the plans I have for you"—this is the Lord's declaration—"plans for your welfare, not for disaster, to give you a future and a hope.~Jeremiah 29:11*

Vision is just one part that makes up the mindset and in the next few chapters we are going to dive into the other things that make up one's mindset. We will look at how we have allowed the things that we have seen, heard, focused on, deem important and the standard we choose to live by dictating to us who we should be, what we can't be and where we fit. Understanding how these things can make us or break us down in the first phase of conception will allow us to fully understand the birthing process so that we can get the conditions right to actually give birth to our purpose.

> *Position Principle: Make a decision from today that you will start to see yourself through the eyes of the one who created you. Look for your value above you not next to you. Know when you are not in alignment with God's vision for your life you will attract pain and hurt, which is a sign.*

~PRAYER FOR VISION~

Father, in the name of Jesus,

I come to you today asking you to help me to see myself the way you see me. Help me to say the things that you say about me. I am struggling with my vision. Help me to have 20/20 vision in the way I see myself and my life. Help me accept myself as I am and to say good things to myself. I often criticize myself so badly, and shrink down in order to fit in. I even dim my light at times so that I won't shine over others. Make my vision plain so I can awaken the creator in me. Reverse the damaging effects of words of discouragement, envy and hate spoken to me and over me. Heal me from past hurts and the disqualifying thoughts that hinder me. Cast out all doubt and fear that paralyze me; thoughts that I am not good enough, smart enough, or simply enough. Clarify the difference between humility and hiding. Heal me from past disappointments and feelings of rejection and abandonment because I am set apart. Wake up the creator inside of me. Awaken the vision you have for me and allow it to match up with my actions and what I say. Give me a clear vision and grant me peace if it doesn't align with what others want for my life. I want to walk in Your complete and perfect will for my life. Help me to be in complete alignment with Your will for my life. Excite me with Your vision for my life.

Help me to listen for Your voice so I can block out all the other voices, even my own. Please help me love myself as I am, to see myself as you see me. From now on, let every action, every word, every reaction, every thought, and every emotion, be based on how you see me. Let the power of your love be present in my whole being that I see myself and everyone through the eyes of your love. Help me that I no longer need to live my life according to other people's expectations and views of me. Today is a new beginning. Help me to start my life over, help me to love you above all and to love myself. Help me to be unapologetic in my pursuit for MORE and view myself and my future through your eyes.

In Jesus name, Amen.

"Finally, brothers and sisters,

whatever is true,

whatever is noble,

whatever is right,

whatever is pure,

whatever is lovely,

whatever is admirable-

if anything is excellent or praise-
worthy- think about such things."

~Philippians 4:8

~CHAPTER 2~

THE ONE THING

Set your mind on things above not things that are on earth. ~Colossians 3:2

I n the Conception Phase, something is actually born. In the natural, conception occurs when a sperm cell from a man joins with the egg of a woman. I would hope by now you would have guessed that we are not discussing the natural birthing process but rather a spiritual one. In spiritual conception, God's purpose for us is joined with our spirit. If our spirit is not strong enough to carry the weight of this purpose it can be miscarried just like in the natural. That is why it can't be stressed enough that it's imperative that you provide the right conditions for it to grow. The Greek word for "born" is translated as Ghennah˙o pronounced (Gen-aw-oh), which actually means from conception to birth. It is also translated as "conceived", which means life begins at conception so one could say spiritual conception begins from the time we are born and develops over time, which requires focus so it can develop properly.

It is during our darkest moments that we must focus to see the light. ~Aristotle

Now let's be honest, as much as I could say I was focused on others, the truth is that I was focused on myself for too long. Although it was masked by others, in all actuality I was focused on my pain and my hurt which obstructed my view as well. Back then, I was focused on everyone else--their goals, their passions, their wants, their needs all because I didn't want to focus on myself. I did not believe in my value. I pushed my friends towards their goals, I was that girl everyone came to if they wanted to get focused but yet I struggled with finding my own focus. I was the girl who helped you build your business, I was the girl that helped you save money, I was the girl that helped you raise your family, I was that girl that helped you focus on the things that you needed to get to your next level but yet I was stuck. I did all of that because I thought I was damaged goods and there was no point in focusing on the greater parts of me because I did not see value in myself. I never knew that there was something that was waiting to be born inside of me. What I have learned is that what you focus on the most is what grows.

Looking back I realize that because I didn't believe I was worthy I focused on everything else but myself. I allowed things that didn't matter to distract me instead of focusing on the things that did matter. Did you know that what you don't pay attention to, is what you actually focus on when you are not intentional? I did not focus on pushing myself harder than my usual growing up. In high school I had a group of friends and we all studied together and of course when studying we talked and played around. I remember getting test scores back and I got a D and some of the other girls got A's and B's. I remember saying to myself how this could be and they told me that after we all went home, they studied again. I felt horrible. I clearly wasn't focusing or paying attention in the way that I should have. I totally missed the mark on that one. It happened to me in many other situations after that. I could have blamed everyone else for what I wasn't doing but the truth is, it was me and what I chose to focus on. Have you ever felt like you missed the mark? What have you been focusing on?

Choose to focus your time, energy and conversation around people who inspire you, support you and help you to grow into your happiest, strongest, wisest self. ~Karen Salmansohn

I was stuck because I allowed things that didn't matter to distract me. Here is the thing, when there is a lack of focus, distraction can creep up without you realizing until it's too late. Because I needed and wanted help, my distraction actually came in the disguise of people. Yes! it's a thing, if you're like me, you are a natural born servant which means you have the heart to give. You find joy in helping others to the point that you would give your last if you had to. Sounds cute, right? Nope! It actually stems from a place of pride. If not done with the right intention and motive you could actually end up hurting yourself. I needed and wanted help so bad because I really wanted someone to help me. The hurt I had now turned itself into pride. Pride says, since no one knew how to help me, I have to help everyone else, I have to be the one that fixes it. I have to be the one who puts everything back together because if I don't, then who will? Because I was still hurt, I didn't realize that I was now attracting people who were users, takers and abusers which was a distraction. I was my biggest distraction.

~The Real Deal~

I thought I forgave, at the moment I did not know what forgiveness was and I definitely did not know the levels of the pain that sat deep inside of me. I didn't even realize I was focusing on the pain and the more energy I gave it the more I lost myself. I was not focused on what was being developed inside of me. I was having miscarriages in the spirit often. I wanted great friends so I became a great friend. I wanted dependable, responsible, loving and caring people I could trust, so I became a trustworthy, dependable, responsible, loving and caring person. All the while I was losing myself because although the intention was good the motive was off. My motive was protecting myself from pain and hurt which meant that not only was I trying to be in control but that I was not vulnerable to life. So in actuality I was a part of the problem as well. Can you think of how you may have played apart in your own demise that came from your pain? I began to realize that in order for me to get more out of my life, I had to focus on me, which meant I would have to actually focus on the one who created me. Weird right? I know but it all makes sense in the end I promise. When I think of things I have put my focus on, I realize that they were detrimental to what God was birthing in me and in an unusual way God allowed everything I went through to work out for my good just as He is doing for you. Every hurt, every affliction, every betrayal will work out in the end for your good in Jesus Christ. I had multiple miscarriages both physically and in the spirit. I was ashamed and felt guilty until I realized it was all to prepare me for the magnitude of what I was really carrying.

You see, God's plan is not our own, His time is not our own and His thoughts are not ours. We have to learn to allow Him to mold us into what His desire is and not our own. My wanting to protect myself and be in control is what constantly led me to being disappointed in others and myself.

"Focus on your strengths, not your weaknesses. Focus on your character, not your reputation. Focus on your blessings, not your misfortunes."
— Roy T. Bennett

~The Teenage Years~

I was a middle child and I always sought attention. There was a point when I even thought I was adopted. I felt misunderstood in my teens. I didn't make sense to anyone I don't even think I made sense to myself. Along with the focus I gave to people I also focused a lot on my emotions and feelings. I spent so much of my teens acting out, looking for attention from the wrong people instead of focusing on the life that I wanted for myself and becoming the person I wanted to be. By the time I realized what was happening, I was a grown woman trapped, lost, and broken. When I look back now I don't even know how I made it through but for the grace of God. Teenage years are very crucial to the development of your mind as well in developing your purpose. I spent the summers of my teenage years either in Barbados or slaving away cooking and selling food at fairs for one of my best friends' mothers. I was asked to help at first and then I was asked to work. I prepared food and prepped for almost 12-18 hours a day as a teen. I was young so I didn't feel the toll it would have had on my body today until years after. Long and short of the story was that all that hard work wasn't for me although I did learn many rules of survival. We were out there every single weekend, driving from state to state, all to help them to buy a home. While I am grateful they were able to purchase a home, I wasn't happy with myself because I didn't put any limit to how much I would "help" so I gave all of me and now I had nothing to show for it. If I had to do it again, I definitely would have done it differently. I would have probably still helped out but on my terms. I definitely put too much focus on other people's happiness and not my own. What are you focusing on right now? How is what you are doing helping you reach your goals?

> *"Look straight ahead, and fix your eyes on what lies before you. Mark out a straight path for your feet; stay on the safe path. Don't get sidetracked; keep your feet from following evil." ~Proverbs 4:25-27*

~Who am I?~

That was me for years, finding myself lost in becoming what everyone else wanted me to be. I was one thing for my parents, another thing for my friends, another thing for my sisters, another for my teachers, another for my boyfriend (which I should absolutely NOT have had anyway because that brought a whole other type of hurt), and another for myself. It got to the point where I just didn't even know who I was. I was probably about six different people depending on who I was around and to be honest it was draining and tiring. I wasn't happy, I was completely lost because I had lost my focus, and I felt like I was a zombie.

At sixteen, I tried to commit suicide and I am NOT proud of this by any means. All I remember is that I just couldn't take it anymore. I knew I was created for more than the life I was living but I didn't believe that I deserved it or that I would ever see it. I felt hopeless and lost. My pain was starting to bury me. One night, I went to a friend's house to talk after I had just broken up with my boyfriend. He had said some really nasty and mean things to me. I had no business having a boyfriend at that time but I wanted to be "grown". I was too young to handle the magnitude of the weight of my emotions, my feelings and his. I wasn't prepared for that level of responsibility as well as the disrespect. I was deeply hurt, I just needed a shoulder to cry on. Again, if I only knew Jesus was my source, I wouldn't have even left my house.

That night I rang her bell and my "ex-boyfriend" stuck his head out the window and said some mean and disgusting things to me and we both started verbally assaulting each other. I didn't understand what he was doing at her house. I couldn't take it anymore, it was as if he poured acid on an open wound. I walked back to my house, sad, confused and hurt. All I could think to myself was, "how could I give someone something they didn't deserve and to be treated like garbage. I gave him a piece of me that I could never get back and I was so mad with myself for that. My mother was nagging me about something as usual when I walked in the house. I didn't even hear her, the pain was so loud. I saw her lips moving but I couldn't hear her. She didn't see the pain and hurt written all over my face. I knew she was talking but I don't even know what she was saying. I was deafened by the pain. I went straight to my room and cried for hours. When everyone went to bed I went downstairs and decided to swallow a bunch of Tylenol and drink it with a bottle of Ammonia. Absolutely crazy, I know. My younger sister saw me fall to the floor and screamed for my mother and that was the last thing I heard before I passed out. My mother said she found me on the kitchen floor, unconscious and called the ambulance and they rushed me to the hospital. I was in and out of consciousness and all I could hear was the doctors telling my mom that they had to pump my stomach. I don't even know if she actually told them what happened. All I heard was the doctor saying that they will report it as food poisoning. Later on I found out that if they had reported what actually happened I would have probably been committed to the psychiatric ward. There was God showing up for me again with His favor, mercy and grace.

I was barely conscious when I had an out of body experience. My mother was crying over me as I was laying in the bed. She was begging God to allow me to wake up and that she would do whatever it was that she had to do if He did. Here was another encounter with God. He saved me once again. That was my first time ever witnessing true repentance. My mother told Him that she would change her life and vow to serve Him for the rest of her life if He allowed me to wake up. Now my mother was a good woman and a great mother but there was more work to be done in her and so she went to God begging

Him that if he allowed me to wake up and live she would not put nothing above Him from that day forward. From the moment I opened my eyes, my mother was never the same again. That was true surrender and obedience. Similar to the prayers of Samson's mother, my mother was willing to give it all up for me. She basically offered me back to Him.

Here is the sad part, I was willing to take my own life for people who didn't even care enough about me to come to the hospital, not even my best friend or my ex-boyfriend. At that time mental health was such a stigma that I don't even think my family knew what I was going through and what happened to me because the doctors just said I had a stomach virus. In our community, depression, suicide and mental health issues were not recognized. Here I was literally dying in front of so many people but they couldn't even see me. It was just me, God and mommy. You see, what I didn't realize was what most of us don't. We are born blessed and we all have a story to tell. God has a purpose for our lives and He will use every good and bad thing that has ever happened to us to His greatness for us. It took me a while to get this and in the process I took my eyes off of Him I lost my bearings and got caught up and even fell on my face a few times.

I definitely learned a lot of lessons from that experience. The biggest lesson I took away from that experience was that my lack of focus could have killed me. I had to learn that I could only be one person and I had to decide who that was and focus on becoming her. I had to learn to be authentically me because everyone else was taken. The day I came out of the hospital I realized that if God didn't allow me to die then, there must be a purpose for me. I decided then that I would choose life from that day forward. I was hurting and I needed somewhere to put the pain so I decided to create. It was after that experience that I learned to use my hands to deal with the wounds of pain, hurt and disappointment. This is when I discovered the gifts of creativity in me. In time it was my creativity that helped to deal with my pain. What do you use to help you cope with your pain?

And he has filled him with the Spirit of God, with skill, with intelligence, with knowledge, and with all craftsmanship, to devise artistic designs, to work in gold and silver and bronze…~Exodus 35:31-32

Creativity became one of my greatest strengths, and equally one of my greatest weaknesses as well. If asked, most creative people would say that they find it very hard to stay focused on one thing. Throughout my life, it was extremely hard for me to stay focused but as creative gifts started to grow, it was even harder. I had so many ideas and visions flowing through my mind at all times, and I didnt know how to manage it all. Imagine not being able to see well in one eye and trying to drive at the same time. That's basically how I lived for many years until

I was set free. I was concerned with so many non-factors that I actually blinded myself, which led to yet another miscarriage. One eye was obstructed because of how I viewed myself and the other eye was blurry because I was concerned with non-factors like having friends, boys and basically all the wrong things that did not matter.

~The Purpose of One~

So although I had many creative talents and gifts, I wasn't able to focus on the purpose for them until I learned to put my focus on the One. The One who inspires--the Original Creator. I can't pinpoint when or how I became so creative, but I do know it was a way to escape my reality. I painted, I knitted, I cooked, I did a lot of art & crafts. Basically I was able to create anything I put my mind to. The love for creating eventually developed a home within the beauty industry. I started with hair, it became talk therapy for me at first. Once my focus changed my life started to change. Although I might have taken my eyes off of Him every now and again His love for me never changed. God is a God of love and forgiveness, and there's never a lost opportunity. What is for you, is for you and it all will work out in His way anyway. Maybe you missed opportunities or found yourself in situations that left you feeling guilty and shameful like me and you feel like you've missed out. Let me be the first to tell you that you haven't. It's all a part of God's plan, but the thing is you have to first tell him you're sorry and make a declaration that you will change and focus on His plan not yours. It's okay, go and talk to Him. Then be silent and listen.

In order to go to the next trimester you need to focus. Focus on who you are and who you are not. We cannot be everything for everyone, when we try to be everything for everyone and we end up burning ourselves out. As a creative woman it's even harder when you burn yourself out because you can't create. You need space and peace to be able to create. If you are a creative like me, pay attention. You will not be able to birth anything in a toxic space. When we are not focusing on the right things we can't make smart decisions. Focus on what God wants for us so that we can be able to see what it is that He's calling us to do. Sometimes we won't even actually see but we will know and trust in Him for our future so you can focus on that. In our lack of focus we also become selfish in that we don't realize what other people around us are going through as well. Not those who want to take from us but those who actually need us. When I chose to hurt myself, I was selfish because I didn't stop to realize that my mother might be going through a lot. Raising three girls, being a wife, working a full time job and going to school was not an easy task. I never stopped to realize that my mother gave up on her dreams so that we could focus on our dreams and goals. Check your motives, are they selfish? Do they need to be realigned?

Commit your work to the Lord, and your plans will be established. ~Proverbs 16:3

In order to focus on God and what He wants for your life you must first practice self- discipline, you will be often misunderstood and that's okay. Establish order in every area of your life- your home, your room, your school, your workplace, your purse- everywhere you can. The number one reason people fail to reach their goals is because of the lack of focus. Take time out for God, put Him as the 1st thing in your day, center yourself with Him. Talk to Him, ask Him what you should put your focus on.

Position Principle: Pay attention to the things that matter. Dismiss everything else. Put your focus on the one thing that controls everything, which is God. Know where you want to go and know where you don't want to go. Be intentional about everything and be unapologetic about it. Have tunnel vision look straight ahead and keep going no matter what.

~PRAYER FOR FOCUS~

Dear Heavenly Father,

Thank you for the gift of thought processes. I submit my focus to you Lord. Thank you. Today I praise you for human minds. Help me to organize my thoughts into strategies and into a plan for completion for your glory. To understand the magnitude of your power is beyond my comprehension, yet every detail of the world is under your care. So Lord, I need your help in learning to trust you completely concerning my life. Silence all the chatter and cancel all distractions that get me off focus. Lord, sometimes my mind grows cloudy with the worries of this world. The fog sets in and I can't think clearly. Everything in my life is not and will not be perfect but I declare I trust you to bring clarity to my mind regarding my life. Help me stay focused on your light in my life. According to Matthew 6:34, "I will not worry about tomorrow, for tomorrow will worry about itself. Each day has enough trouble of its own." Help me not to get caught up in worry. Help me to keep my eyes focused on you Father because my steps are ordered by you. Would you provide clarity as I surrender all my plans to You. I come against every attack that has been sent to "deter, destroy, and distract" my clarity and focus in any form. Give me keen discernment so I can decipher what my focus should be on and in which season. I lay down worry, anxiety and misplaced focus. I trust You to work everything that I need in my favor and in perfect timing. I pray for fresh clarity and a renewed focused daily.

In Jesus' name, Amen

"I'm not saying that I have this all togeth-er, that I have it made. But I am well on my way, reaching out for Christ, who has so wondrously reached out for me. Friends, don't get me wrong: By no means do I count myself an expert in all of this, but I've got my eye on the goal, where God is beckoning us onward—to Jesus. I'm off and running, and I'm not turning back.

So let's keep focused on that goal, those of us who want everything God has for us. If any of you have something else in mind, something less than total commitment, God will clear your blurred vision—you'll see it yet! Now that we're on the right track, let's stay on it."

~Philippians 3:12-16

~CHAPTER 3~

DO NOT GIVE UP!

And not only that, but we also glory in tribulations, knowing that tribulation produces perseverance, and perseverance, character; and character hope. ~ Romans 5:3-4

The Conception Phase is all about the conditions. If the conditions are not right the fetus (our purpose) cannot grow. The conditions are the experiences, lessons and people we interact with, whether it be once or daily it will ultimately nurture your purpose or try to kill it. Our body was made to function together and when something comes against its function it automatically goes into protection mode and begins to malfunction which leads to a fight against itself causing a release, in this case a miscarriage. It fights off whatever is threatening it even if it is itself. Autoimmune diseases like hypothyroidism, lupus, rheumatoid arthritis and many others decrease the body's ability to fight invaders which make our bodies vulnerable to infections. The body loses its senses in knowing what is good or bad for it and so it just begins to fight and so we lose both what is good and bad for our bodies. On the other hand, whether the conditions are right meaning that everything is in alignment, then we are able to birth infinite possibilities through our purpose. But don't lose hope. God will still use every condition to help us to give birth.

~Life Lessons~

Growing up, I relied on three things to get me through daily- grit, tenacity and resilience and to this day I still use these tools as I have become a spiritual warrior for the kingdom. Grit is what I wake up with, tenacity gets me through the day and resilience is what I go to bed with. Even though I did not know Him well, God knew me and still gave me gifts that would one day be used for His glory. These three traits keep me going when I feel like giving up. When I had nothing else I had these tools that would strengthen me in ways I could never explain and little did I know that my spirit was protecting my purpose the whole time. Isn't God good? Even when you don't see Him, He sees you.

Like most teenagers, I had a love-hate relationship with my mom, partially because she just knew it all and I did not want to admit it. Funny enough, she was always right and I just couldn't stand that. In the midst of our tumultuous relationship, she was able to teach me many things. I have always had a desire for wisdom as well as knowledge. Being teachable is key to growth. My mother dropped gems of wisdom on me almost everyday. As the middle child, I just felt as if I didn't fit in. My sisters and I didn't like the same things so I often found myself alone with my thoughts or with my Mom. Funny thing is, we didn't always agree but I loved to hang out with her. The wisdom she imparted and continues to impart is priceless. Thank God she never took me seriously and always prayed for me. Eventually as I found God, I found myself and He mended things between all five of us. We have learned to embrace and love each other in our differences and that is a major condition that we needed.

Now that I am an adult I am so grateful for those years of isolation when I was younger. It allowed me time to get to know myself and to be trained by life. One of the many things that my mother taught me was that can't wasn't a word. I remember when I was younger, I used to say, "I can't do this." And she would always ask, "What'd you say?" The more I said " I can't", the more she would ask, "what did you say?" until I finally said I CAN do it. She would only acknowledge me when I said I COULD do it. She corrected me by saying, "you can say I can do it, but it's a little difficult" or "It's a little hard, but I can do it." Never tell yourself you can't because once you tell yourself you can't, you won't. I took those words with me into adulthood. So when people look at the things that I create and ask "Is there anything you can't do?" I always say "No!" I live by those words. I eventually learned that it was because of Christ who strengthens us and not because of myself. It doesn't matter what happens in life, I know that I can get through it. She taught me that I could do anything with God by my side.

In this life, you have to be able to push yourself when you think you can't. Grit, tenacity, and resilience cannot be taught, it can only be cultivated through life's wilderness moments and we have many of them. It is only through Jesus that we receive supernatural strength. When Jesus was in the wilderness for forty days that He was tempted by the devil but it was also there that He learned that He could defeat him. We can because He did.

Never stop fighting until you arrive at your destined place - that is, the unique you. Have an aim in life, continuously acquire knowledge, work hard, and have the perseverance to realize the great life.
~A. P. J. Abdul Kalam

Remember if it were easy, everyone would do it. Who ever said the birthing process was ever going to be easy. If you didn't know, it comes with many levels of pain and hurt in preparation for the process. It is very uncomfortable and it stretches you in ways that you can ever imagine. Not to mention when you give your life to the Lord for real. Birthing your purpose comes with a level of persecution that no one really talks about. The thing is, it's all about how you look at a situation and what you decide to focus on. Do you look at the glass as half empty or do you look at it as half full? Are you focused on the fact that you have a glass to drink or are you focused on the fact that there is not a lot of water in the glass. Take a moment to think about everything you have been through, your wilderness moments. Have you allowed those moments to make you bitter or better? If you have been bitter perhaps it is because you don't know why these moments are happening.

~Your Why~

Knowing is half the battle, it makes a huge difference. There is something in all of us that makes us get up and fight everyday and that is what helps us birth our purpose. The problem is most of us don't know why we do what we do. We grew up with people telling us who and what we are and we never questioned it. Then we become adults, living mundane lives with tedious daily routines and before we know it we retire from jobs that we didn't like and we eventually die with our purpose still inside of us. We basically end up living like functioning zombies, doing the least to get minimal results. Barely living out the intention God had created for us. Some of us try to navigate out of the norm but still end up short because we lose sight of the goal, halfway through. Then there are some of us, like you and me, who know there is more to us and more to our lives. That there is something great inside of us and are willing to do what it takes to bring it out. We have made a decision that it's not about what we are going through at the moment but we focus on the fact that we will get through. What makes us different is that we know why.

Ultimately our passions and purposes may be different but our "Why" is the same. We must know that we are called, commissioned and chosen to spread the gospel of Jesus Christ in and through our lives in every way. Again, this can be achieved through many different ways but the fact remains that we don't get up because of our own desires but because we have business to do that is not our own. Putting it that way gave me a little more perspective in the way I handle things. Knowing that there is nothing that I do that makes me "right" or "good" but it is everything about who God is helps me to always remember it's "never" about me. Thinking like this allowed me to develop something called grit, which is courage and strength of character. The reality is, if you think you can do it on your own you won't get very far in life. When I was younger I wanted to be a model and I remember an agency saying to me "it's not just about beauty, and it's not not just about talent, it's about the right combination of both. The right combination will keep you in the rooms and allow you to be able to persevere through whatever life brings you". No matter what I did, no matter what I was trying to do, once Jesus was with me and working through me all would be.

~Going Through~

I can remember some points in my life where I had to persevere under the circumstances given to me all the while never realizing that God was cultivating and preparing the conditions for me to give birth. One Sunday afternoon when I was about 11 years old, we came home from church, and my sisters and my mom were in the living room watching Colombo. My oldest sister was reading a book. My younger sister was on the floor just playing around. I decided that that was too boring for me so I went into the kitchen and told my mother I was going to cook and she said, fine, go ahead. I was the type of child who always went above and beyond and so I wanted to cook a five course meal. I don't even remember what I cooked. I just remember that it was a 5 course meal with all of the extras included- menu cards, candlelight, all of that. I went into the kitchen to light the candles and I had the menu cards in my hand and one card dropped. My hair was pulled back in a ponytail and I turned to pick up the card on the floor and all I heard was snap, crackle and pop. Literally I got up and turned towards the window, which showed a reflection of flames. All I could see was a fire blazing on the back of my head, I couldn't believe what I was looking at, so I just calmly said, "Mom". I said it about three times when my mother who was in between sleep finally heard me and turned to me and kind of opened one eye. When she saw what was happening, she literally leapt from the chair. She flew into the kitchen and doused my head into a sink full of dishes and all. Thank God I had long hair. I basically had about half a ponytail left after the flame was put out. If you didn't know me personally, you wouldn't even have known that this happened. It just looked like I just cut my hair, it happened so fast that I do not remember being afraid. I just remember my mom telling me, "girl, you scared me" and my sisters honestly busting out laughing because they just thought it was the biggest joke and we laughed about it. I truly believe because of how my mother handled the situation, it never bothered me. It didn't stop me from going back into the kitchen the next week. I just knew I had to be smarter by making better choices. When I think of tenacity, I think of situations like that. No matter what it may look like, no matter what you've gone through, if you determine in your mind to get things done, and to push through then that's all that matters. Is there something that you have gone through that felt like hell but you know it was pushing you to be better? This helps to prepare the conditions to give birth to your purpose.

"Consider it pure joy my brothers and sisters whenever you face trials of many kinds, because you know that the testing of your faith produces perseverance" ~James 1: 2-3

There are many times I could think of throughout my lifetime that I had to push past horrible circumstances to get to the other side. While I was going through it I didn't see what

God was trying to develop in me. Reflecting back it was in those times my faith was developing and would be the secret weapon that has gotten me from one level to the next. Trying to do things on your own, fueled by pain and disappointment can send you into a valley of chaos which makes you spiritually abort your purpose because the conditions are not right. I have had many spiritual abortions becuse I did not know who I was and therefore I was not in the correct alignment for me to birth what God has put in me. Although I couldn't give birth, God was using what I was going through to develop the proper conditions so that when the time was right I would be ready. I first had to be challenged because of my stinking thinking. Even in the midst of wrongdoing, God still can use a bad situation for His glory. God allowed me to go through a horrific situation to teach me the magnitude of what I had inside of me. You are stronger than you think too.

~Broken Pieces~

One time that sticks out in my mind that really defines how God was able to develop my faith in the midst of my messiness was when I was a lost, confused young teenager. I was a rebellious teen and that led me down a dark path that led to rejection, abandonment, shame and guilt. It was a sunny afternoon in the spring and I was freaking out. My mind was racing and I was scared. I went by my friend's house to take a pregnancy test. I remember standing out on her porch, crying my eyes out because I knew my life was over. Yes, I had premarital sex, and that decision sent me down a hard and painful road. This was my choice and I made a poor choice. The test was positive and I was frozen. If I had this baby, I knew that my parents would be disappointed in me and I was even more disappointed in myself. I knew that this was not what my life was supposed to be. Now, I know that only God gives and takes life but I also knew that this was not my life. I am not trying to make anyone who got pregnant at a young age feel bad. I just knew that this was not God's plan for me. I also knew the father and I were teenagers with no jobs. In the midst of what I was going through, he started to show me his true colors. My vision was still distorted but for some reason it started clearing up now. I was starting to see my life for what it really was, that what was happening to me was a distraction from the very beginning. I will explain more later. After what felt like years of turmoil but it was actually days, I decided I was not going to have a baby. As scared as I was, I knew in my heart that this wasn't for me and that was my peace in this situation. I couldn't tell anyone so it was just God and me. That decision was the start of World War 7 for me. The coming weeks were hell. My boyfriend told me that he had to tell the truth and that I was messing up his plan for our lives. He said, he poked holes in the condom on purpose to get me pregnant so I would be with him forever. I couldn't believe the words that were coming out of his mouth. That was devastating. I was so angry and hurt. Why would someone purposely plot to hurt me intentionally? I couldn't seem to wrap my head around it for a very long time. I was so hurt, and to add insult to injury he became very mean. He started to be very disrespectful and abusive verbally and physically. He called me every hurtful name in the book. He even told me that I was going to go to hell if I aborted his baby.

The day that I decided to go in and have the procedure done, I asked God to forgive me. I skipped school and then went on an interview for my summer job that same day. I was so scared and nervous and I just honestly, wanted my mommy, but because I knew she would be disappointed in me, I couldn't tell her. All I remember is waking up after the procedure to someone banging on the door. It was my boyfriend screaming and cursing me out and spewing hurtful things. He was screaming that I was a baby killer, that I would go to hell. The nurses asked me if I felt safe to go home with him. I went home feeling ashamed, rejected, disappointed and unworthy. I wore those clothes of shame for many, many years until years later when the Lord showed me that I didn't have to live like that. The most hurtful thing about this entire process was that I had to come home and pretend like everything was okay. My mother didn't know about this until I was well into my twenties. I look back now and thank God for the ability to persevere through it all. I eventually learned that I was already forgiven and that He could still use me for His glory. Please note it was a process. It didn't happen overnight. It took time for me to be cleaned up for the conditions to be right for me to come to terms with what God was birthing in me. Through it all though I had faith that I wouldn't have to live like that forever. Is there something that makes you feel shame & guilt? Are you wearing those clothes and don't even realize it? The only way for you to actually birth your purpose is to actually get intimate with God. He sees you and still loves you. He wants to use you but you have to get out of the way. There is nothing He can't do. The question is will you let Him? Do you have faith that it can get better?

> *"Faith is like film, it only gets developed in the dark." ~Dr. Rev. Lashley*

Please note once you have made it through the Conception phase, you are well on your way. Know that nothing is impossible for God. God can use the messiest person for His glory. Don't believe what people have said, God loves you and He always will. There is nothing too bad for God. Like I told you earlier, if He could see me and love me, despite my messiness, He can see you too. It's all about you letting Him. The Conception phase happens when life first begins, so we have to be careful in letting the things we see and hear make up our mindset. Our mindset establishes how we perceive things and react to things. Take a moment and look at the things that have shaped your thinking. Not just what you've been through, but what you were exposed to as well. What are you exposing yourself to now? You know there is more but before you can get to the MORE, you have to be willing to own the fact that you have made poor choices and remove the "victim" mentality. It's not what happened to you but rather why did it happen to you. I've come to realize that it's all about perspective. In every situation, trial and tribulation there are always two things that come out of it- a blessing and a lesson.

Position Principle: Your circumstance does not define you. Despite what your story is, know that there is more for you. It doesn't end here. Keep going! God has a plan for your life even if you don't see it. Always remember the longest rope has an end... just don't let go!

~PRAYER FOR PERSEVERANCE~

Dear Father God,

I thank you for grace in the midst of trials. I have a desire for greatness, not for myself but for your glory. Show me how to shift my thinking so I can see that all that I have been through was for me and not against me. In your power I can persevere through anything. I dream of so much more for myself that I know it can't be me. Help me to fight, even against myself if I must for your purposes and plans for my life to prevail. Grant me an incredible tenacity to complete the tasks put before me. Grant me grit to push through what looks impossible. Stir up a resilience in me that can stand through every situation or person sent to make me fail. Allow my grind to be a graceful grind covered in humility. I want to be an unstoppable force for Your kingdom. I cancel the power of failure and hindrance over my life by the blood of Jesus. I confess that sometimes I allow the dreariness of the world to stop me from seeing things the way you do. I declare and decree that today is a new day and that I have enough faith to get me through each day. I ask that you grant me new ideas, new energy, new determination and new insight. Help me to make every day I live to count for something in Your kingdom. I want to live everyday as if it were my last. Help me to take full accountability for my life and the decisions I've made. In Your perfect timing, I surrender my will for my life and wait in patience. Teach me to hear your voice so I will know when to make a move and to know what it will require from me. May you grant me perseverance in not only strength but wisdom, knowledge and understanding. I call for the spirit of might to reign over me even now. Give me a complete fullness of joy for what I do daily. May my perseverance count me worthy in your eyes, so I can complete the race for Your glory.

In Jesus' Name,

Amen

Phase 2: Transition

THE TREASURED YEARS

"Nothing great was ever done without adapting, adjusting and avoiding!"

Growth is often
uncomfortable, messy,
and full of feelings you
weren't expecting.
But it's necessary!
~unknown

~CHAPTER 4~

IT DOES NOT FIT

When I was a child, I spoke as a child, I understood
as a child, I thought as a child; but when I became a
man, I put away childish things.
~1 Corinthians 13:11

In Phase Two of the Divine Birthing Process, The Transition Stage, which I call "The Treasured Years," our beliefs, character and identity are stretched to show us who we really are. In this phase more will be required from you so you must be willing to do different things to get different results. Every person must go through a transition phase at some point in their life in order for growth to occur and every person's phase is completely different. Mine lasted a very long time because I did everything in my power to control it. Waking up, feeling confused every day, not knowing if you can truly be who you were destined to be, not being true to your authentic self is something that can definitely send you into a world wind of depression. I suffered from depression for a long time. From the time I knew myself as a teenager into my adult years, I suffered from an unexplainable sadness. For the most part I was able to hide it and sometimes it consumed me. All I could do was pretend I was sick and cry until I was able to fight my way out. It took me a long, long time to walk in who I was unapologetically. It took me a long time to become who I am now and become who I was called to be and still journeying to be, because it's a journey and not a destination. Through discovering God, I was able to find truth, identity and my purpose. In my journey to discovering God, I actually had to learn to be myself. A trait you need to learn if you are going to survive in this world. In the beginning, I compromised who I was and adjusted to whatever it was that people needed me to be, even if it meant not being who they wanted me to be. This phase is actually one of the most painful because it requires a stretching of your physical, mental, emotional strength. It also requires an unexplainable amount of faith to get you through to the other side. In this phase God requires your full attention. It is also one of the most uncomfortable times of your life. I was a complete mess. I don't want you to think that it just happened for me. I had to continuously get into position because I kept forgetting who I was, until I finally made a decision to fight for me. There's a shift that happens and it occurs inside of you in your mind and in your spirit when you make a choice. It can feel like pressure is on all sides. But remember, God is actually preparing you for the labor process so He has to make sure you can handle the pressure of giving birth..

~I Am... ~

It took a long time for me to become aware of myself and who I actually wanted to be. I was one person from my friends, a different person for my parents, another for my boyfriends, another for my employees, and another for my teachers. Thank God I did not grow up in the era of social media because that's another type of beast. I was a complete mess. You might have thought that I always had it together but I didn't. I just looked like I did. We all transition in the physical from girl to woman and there is also a transition that happens in the spirit as well that most of us don't talk about. The transition from a baby believer to a mature believer. The difference between the physical and the spiritual transition is that because the spiritual is not evident by a person's capability to see and touch like the physical, some of us never transition and that keeps us stuck spiritually, emotionally and mentally. The willingness to grow spiritually and develop personally, prepare you to take the next steps so you can give birth. This transition occurs inside of you, inside of your mind, inside of your spirit, so you can safely give birth to your purpose. The transition phase is challenging because there is a shift happening that is not easy to put into words. It's actually something that you don't understand at the moment. The pressure on all sides can feel unbearable.

Let's discuss the meaning of purpose by definition. Purpose is the reason for which something exists. If you are reading this book, you too believe that we all were born with a purpose, given by the creator himself, God and that each person has a different purpose. Understand that it takes the right conditions and time to be able to birth out one's purpose. I also believe that purpose is not a one size fits all, like a fetus develops into a baby, purpose develops from identity. Knowing that, it's safe to say that most times we can't birth our purpose because we don't know our identity. For as long as I can remember I was the person everybody wanted me to be and the burden of that was slowly killing me, literally. I struggled because I didn't know who I was. I was always in a deep depression so much so I just thought that was life. I was making myself sick, I suffered from migraines, constant body & joint pain, brain fog, lack of concentration, couldn't gain weight and the list goes on. Every doctor I went to couldn't connect the symptoms. They sent me for test after test.

It was at the point I had given up, God swept in and saved me from myself, there was an answer finally. By the age of twenty-one I was clinically diagnosed with an autoimmune disease called hypothyroidism, adrenal deficiency, rheumatoid arthritis, depression. Basically my thyroid gland had given up on me. The thyroid controls many other glands in your body and it basically controls the level of stress your body can handle. The adrenal gland, which controls the "fight or flight" responses, gave up on me too. The doctors told me at the rate I was going I would probably have cancer in a few years if I didn't have it already. They sent me to have more tests and x-rays done. My levels were all over the place, I was on so many medications to try to stabilize my body. My body was literally fighting me. Needless to say it wasn't looking good. Thank God, it took about two years before my body would come under subjection and begin to work with me and not against me. I did not have cancer but I sure felt like I did, I did have to be put on multiple medications for the rest of my life. The doctors told me that because my body was fighting itself, there was a strong possibility that I wouldn't be able to conceive. Everyday I felt like it was going to be my last, I cried all day, everyday. I have never endured so much constant pain. While most people dreamt of fancy cars, money and clothes, I dreamt of living with no pain, physically living life, laughing with friends, going to the park... but everyday I awoke to being confined to a bed all day because everything hurt. In my mind I knew that was not going to be my reality but my body had not gotten the picture yet.

I asked myself how I got here and I realized for a long time the burden of being who everyone wanted me to be was slowly killing me. I was in such a state of deep depression thought that was life. Here I was just becoming an adult, becoming my own woman at twenty-one and I got hit with this news that threw me upside down, literally. It wasn't making any sense to me.

~Know This~

For my entire life I gave of myself to everyone but me, and now that I needed to show up for myself, I was nowhere to be found. My new reality sent me on a downward spiral but thanks to my mother and God, it wasn't too long before I was able to get up and fight. I had to fight through the depression, fight through the sickness and fight for my life. My Mom was my commander at that time. She was such a strength. She told me, "I had to get up and take back my life." She would say, "you're not dead so what's the plan?" Harsh, I know but that's what I needed to hear. She gave me scriptures in the book of Psalms to say and truth be told many days I lied and told her I said it when I didn't. She also gave me her Bible and a prayer book, The Warfare Prayer Book, volumes 1 & 2, by Kenneth Scott, that I still use today. At first I was upset that she was even talking to me like that and I would always ask the point of these prayers. My spirit was discouraged. I told her God couldn't hear me anyway. But one night, after I really prayed I heard a soft voice as I was crying myself to sleep saying, "I created you for more." If you were supposed to die, you would have, I did not create you to suffer. You suffer because of the decisions you've made. You can trade suffering for freedom in me, if you want to but it's all up to you. No matter what you choose, I will always love you!"

Immediately I stopped crying, I knew that was God. I thought of how I was pitying myself. Then I started to cry because I knew what time it was, I knew what I had to do. That night I made up my mind that I was going to fight my way out with the help of God. I believe I developed something in me that I never had before, a fight of resilience grew in me. I became "the original bounce back kid" that night. God then activated a fight in me that was not going to come from my own strength but His. I realized that it was not my time to die and if He woke me up one more time each day, I was going to fight everyday and live like it was going to be my last. I was tired of being tired and there had to be a way out. My mother was my advocate and still is today, she told me, "Nadia, I can't fight for you but I will fight with you because you are not in this alone" and we have been fighting everyday since then. Having my mom and God was all I needed and I began to move. Now you might have or you might not have your mother but you do have God and he comes as a three person deal, Father, Son and Holy Spirit. Because you are reading this book, you now have me, your Treasured Midwife, to help you along the way. Know that you were created for more. Your circumstances don't define you, your environment doesn't define you, even your thoughts and actions don't define you, Jesus defines you.

~Me, Me, Me~

My mom brought out the resiliency that God put in me, and we decided that we were going to fight. It wasn't easy at all at first I had to change my thinking about everything I was ever taught in life. That included the foods I ate, what I listened to and watched, the people I allowed around me, the way I saw God, the way I saw myself and thought about life in its entirety. The leader in me had to assess how I got here, which was a harsh reality to face. I had to admit to myself that I was here because of me. Was it my fault alone? No, but I had a part to play in it because it was my life. I wanted to be in control at all times. Because of what happened to me at thirteen, here I was making decisions from that pain which is what led to me getting sick. I was not only harboring the pain from what happened, but over the years other things like unforgiveness, anger, rage, rejection, abandonment and much more attached to it like a magnet.

Here I was faced with blockage after blockage. Eventually I realized it was my pride. Let me break it down. Pride says it's all about me. Yes, there is a harsh reality of pride that we all know of but there is also a subtle reality of pride that most of us have but it's hidden and only comes out in ways that you won't even look at if you're not paying attention. Being in "control" is a cover for pride as well as "helping" people. Here is what I mean, not all help is "good" help. What is the real reason behind why you want to help people? What are the motives and intentions? I had to realize that although I wanted to help people, the real reason why I wanted to help them was because I needed help myself. Since no one was able to help me, I figured I could be that person to help everyone. Thinking like that takes away God's job because He is put into a box and you end up hurting yourself like I did. He created us in His image. He is our Father and he is the person to go to for help. Understanding that concept took me some time and as I was growing through it, God was transitioning me as He was preparing me for labor and delivery. Honestly, I feel that this was God's way of getting my attention. I sometimes feel honored because it could have been worse. The way I see it, dealing with my heart is my "bitter cup" or "my cross" that I have to bear, to remind me that I am human and that I need God. People look at me and want to be me, they see my obedience to God but what they don't know is that I have had to count the costs. It took a lot to be here.

To be honest, some days I struggle, I still have attacks and I don't want to hear anything, I just want to feel normal. On those days I run to God and I stay in His presence for as long as needed to. Please note that I am not telling these stories for pity. I am using my story to help you. Please don't just read this book just to read but ask if you can see yourself in me. Are there some decisions that you've made or you're making that are not so smart? Is there a choice that you're making right now that you know will end up hurting you?

Here is what I learned throughout my journey a little late. Take responsibility for your life because no one else will. In life, growth is necessary and there will be times you will have to adapt and adjust to the way God wants in the process. Growth is something I had to learn the hard way. My mother was right about everything- my friends, my life, my career. She was right about pretty much every single thing that I went through in life because she saw me and she was put as the head over me. God is a God of order and believes in authority. We tend to want to come out of order because we think we know it all. I had to learn through too many bad situations that I didn't know it all. I had to understand that my mother was right and not just my mother but those God had put in my life to guide me. Maybe your mother might not be the one, but trust that God has put someone in your life to cover you. Ask yourself if you know who that is and if you don't ask Him to reveal them to you? If you know who is your covering, do you listen to what they say over your life or do you do your own thing because you think you know best? I had to learn the hard way and was forced to give up my right to be right or die. In all that I have gone through, it is as simple as that. It could have gone another way. Ask God to reveal right counsel, from your Pastor, spiritual mother, biological mother or other. Sit under wisdom and knowledge. Don't seek to be seen but rather to hear. Growth is a process.

Position Principles: Grow up.

Growth requires two abilities.

The ability to listen clearly and the ability to follow directions.

Failure is a part of growing as well, it's all a part of the process.

It is in the commitment to grow that will birth success.

~PRAYER FOR GROWTH~

Dear Heavenly Father,

Thank you for choosing me, Thank you for calling me, Thank you for saving me. Without your grace I do not know where I would be. Lord, I ask you to fill me with the knowledge of Your will in my life. I come to you today Lord for spiritual wisdom and understanding, so I can walk in my life, fully pleasing You. Bearing fruit in everything I do.

I want to evolve into the woman you have called me to be. Forgive me father for putting my own needs, wants and desires before you. Lord help me to turn away from the world's definition of what I should look like.

Grant me the serenity to accept the things I cannot change; the courage to change the things I can; and the wisdom to know the difference.[1]

Help me to humble my heart and my spirit Lord. Correct anything in me that is delaying my growth. Change me in the ways that I need to change to handle what you're birthing in me. Blow my mind with your favor. I pray for your calming peace to come over me as I grow in this transition of my life. Help me to see the good that will rise from this. Instead of worrying and looking through the eyes of anxiety, I choose to pray and have faith that Your perfect will be done even if I can't see it. I trust

1 The Serenity Prayer, Reinhold Niebuhr

that You are molding me, and pressing me down on all sides so that I can be in direct alignment with Your perfect plan for my life.

In Jesus Name, Amen.

~CHAPTER 5~

YOU GOT THIS!

We are hard-pressed on every side, yet not crushed;
we are perplexed, but not in despair; persecuted, but
not forsaken; struck down, but not destroyed—
~2 Corinthians 4:8-9

Transition is something we all have to go through, but I don't think we realize what it takes to actually go through the physical and mental levels involved. We have our thoughts of what our life might look like, but the reality is that we have no idea. We also think we have a choice and the reality is that we don't. Only God knows what our full purpose is and only He gives us the strength to be able to go through what it is that we need to go through. You might be feeling as if you're in a storm all by yourself and that there is no sign of hope or dry land in sight. You are wandering through life living day to day knowing you will find your way but not knowing when it looks impossible. What you and I didn't realize is that all we need is to focus on the one thing that will help us through and that one thing is named Jesus. Only through Him, can God give us strength and endurance to get through when needed. With Jesus every next step is possible. When you're lost and unsure like I was, His wisdom will show you a path through. You just have to listen for Him. I was living life to the beat of my own drum until it burst and there was silence until I heard His voice clearly through the hardest battles of my life.

~A Blessing In the Lesson~

Another time I heard Him was in my late twenties, still struggling with hypothyroidism, but I was doing okay. For the most part, life was good. I was getting adjusted to my life, my new normal when my boyfriend at the time and I broke up. It was not his fault, it was actually mine. I cheated on him. He really loved me but he couldn't forgive me and I understood. I hurt him really badly and I vowed to myself after that not to ever hurt someone like that ever in life. I realized hurt people hurt people. I was hurting so badly that I ran into the arms of another man, battered and bleeding both in the spirit and metaphorically. I just wanted to erase my life and forget all that I had been through. All the fights, all the hurt, all the pain. Instead of dealing with my issues, I ran into the arms of another man.

He was a mirror image of me and I didn't realize it until it was too late. All I wanted was to be loved and feel worthy. Before I knew it, I was engaged. I cried like a baby the night I got engaged. It was crazy because everyone was so happy for me but I knew something wasn't right. I knew something was wrong. I did not know what was wrong but I knew it in my gut. Trust your gut, it's God trying to get your attention. I stayed and hoped the feeling would go away. Here I was again, trying to be something I wasn't. I wasn't ready to be anybody's wife. Before I could get out, I was pregnant. This time I was different though, so I decided to keep the baby. After being told I couldn't have children, I owed God at this point because He came through for me by allowing me to conceive even though I wasn't trying. I never dreamt about marriage but I always dreamt about being someone's mother. I just knew I would have a little girl that looked just like me. The doctors said that I would not be able to bring the baby to term and if I did, the child would be born with deformities. But despite what the circumstances were, God made a way. We decided that I was going to wean myself off of the synthetic medication that I was told I would have to take for the rest of my life to a lower dose plant based medication for my thyroid. My faith kicked in and I knew we were going to be alright. I changed my entire diet and daily routines. Eventually I got off of all medication after giving birth to a healthy baby girl.

~The Awakening~

There is always a lesson and a blessing in times of trials and tribulations. The journey of bringing her into this world was not easy. There was an unexplainable bond between her and I.

It was the same with my second born son. Both of them were definitely destined to be here. My first child was my way back to God. She was another wake up call that I had a purpose to birth. She was my 1st gift from God that allowed me to see myself for the first time. It was definitely not an easy pregnancy, or engagement. I fainted in my second trimester and so I had to move back in with my parents. That was very hard to go back but I learned that sometimes God uses what looks like a setback as a set up for His glory. I was on bed rest throughout most of that pregnancy so I had a lot of down time to really see who I was and who I wanted to be. I had time to think about what kind of mom I wanted to be and I realized that I was not happy with who I was looking at in the mirror.

Scars are not a sign of weakness, they are signs of survival and endurance ~Rodney A. Winters

All I knew was I couldn't settle. I knew I wasn't born to be in a box. I knew that there was just so much more for my life and I was willing to die for it. I tried my hardest to make things work but they just didn't. Before I knew I became a single mother seven months later. That was very hard and again here I was a total disappointment to myself not realizing I was never a disappointment to God. I could not wrap my head around being a single mom, a title I never wanted to have. But there I was, not only a single mom but a single mom with a health condition that affected my mental stability as well. More importantly, I was a new mom, who had no clue on how to be a mom. Good thing God has the foresight of knowing my end before my beginning. Moving back home gave me the support I needed. The thought of knowing someone else was in the house really helped me to keep my mind as sane as possible through this transition. God always knows the why and the when. He knows what it takes to force you into the realization that there is something inside of you that has to come out but first, you have to acknowledge that there is something there. I had to adapt to my new reality which meant seeing myself for who I really was and not what everyone else saw or even what I pretended to see. I had to ask myself daily, what I was hiding even from myself. This is a question that I could not answer for a long time.

Coming back home was hard enough but coming back with a baby and single felt even worse. It was a hard battle and in the midst of now being responsible for someone else I was losing it. I felt hopeless, anxious, scared, lonely, depressed, sad and still had to take care of my baby. The first few months were very difficult. Her father and I fought about everything from the very beginning. We fought about the air. We fought about clothes. We fought about life. We fought over small things, big things, dumb things, sensible things, bad things, good things, all things. I could not fathom the thought that the world that I saw for myself, what I wanted for myself, all came crashing down.

~It's Time to Activate~

I remember going into my mother's bedroom one night, I was a complete mess. She was laying on her bed and looked up at me and said, "Are you ready to tie up your waist and pull up your bootstraps? What are you going to do? To this day, these are some of the most powerful words that catapulted me to where I am now. I keep them in my "Treasure Vault of Wisdom", where I keep all the impartations I have learned over the years. I know it might sound harsh, but it was such a quick gut wrenching punch, that I could do nothing, except to stand up, wipe my tears, and go to God about what my next steps were going to be. In that moment, all I could do was grow up.

My childhood was very rough in the sense that my parents were very hard on me. They were very strict and harsh at times. They always told me how it was, straight, no chaser. I absolutely hated it but they must have known that I would be able to handle it. As I got older I realized that they were also preparing me for life. It taught me how to endure through the hard times and push past what seemed like the never ending hardships of life. The separation from the father of my child tore me apart because it tore my family apart but built me up for what life was going to deal me in the next few years. What my mother told me was that I was going to have to figure this out. As much as my parents were there for moral support they were not going to be taking care of me and my child. I gave up the victim role and the shame and guilt of being a single mom and realized I was not alone. But it wasn't smooth sailing for me. God was with me even when I didn't know He was there and even when I didn't want him to be. It took a long time before I truly accepted Him into my heart again. I ran away from Him before because I was angry, hurt and disappointed that I was in this position in my life.

It's crazy because as I look back, I have to laugh because how could I be angry with God for where I put myself? I was so mad because I knew there was more for me but with everything going on, how was I going to ever get it. One afternoon I was with my daughter and I decided that was it for me, I was throwing in the towel. She had bad colic and she basically cried all night and day. I was exhausted, hungry and hurting. I couldn't do it anymore. I put my daughter in the middle of my bed, got dressed and left. My mother was downstairs and she kept calling my name as I pulled out the driveway. I could not stop, I just knew I had to get out of there fast. I drove up to the outpatient mental part of the hospital, parked and went inside. I literally told them to lock me up because I was a bad mother. They put me in a bare room and had me wait there until a doctor could see me. I felt so bad, I did not deserve to be a mother. Soon the doctors came with the nurse and asked me a bunch of questions. They immediately asked me if I hurt the baby which I didn't. When they asked me if I wanted to hurt myself, I couldn't answer. They told me I had something called postpartum depression. I never even heard of that. All I knew was that I was in a very dark place and I did not see a way out. They told me they would prescribe some pills and that I needed rest and if I still felt the same way to come back. I left the hospital and went to fill the prescription. I felt like a walking zombie. No feeling, no purpose, no point to my existence. When I finally got the pills I just stared at them not knowing if I should really take them or not. I turned my phone off and drove around for hours. I finally stopped driving and I let it all out in the car. I screamed and cried for as long as I could. When I could not cry anymore I heard a voice saying to me, "You have to fight. You have to keep moving." It was a calming, soothing yet stern voice. I knew it was God. He didn't bring me that far just to bring me that far.

~The White Flag~

I wiped my face, took a deep breath and went back home to my baby. Most of my family doesn't even know that story. I shared it to encourage someone reading right now. You may want to give up, everything in you wants to throw in the towel. You can't see past what you're going through right now. But, I am here to tell you, you can. You just have to keep moving. Don't stay in your pain, don't sit in your disappointment. When I got back in the house my parents were so worried. They told me if I took those pills I may never come back. That night I emptied the bottle of pills in the toilet and that was when I decided to fight. I was going to fight my way out. I kissed my baby girl and I asked her to forgive me. I promised her and myself I would never leave her or myself again. Now, I am not saying life after that was easy peasy because it wasn't. Depression was on the back of my heels like sand is to water but with prayers that my mom gave me to say like Psalms 3, 23, 26, 52, 91, 119 and some others, I was able to make it through. From that night on, I kept moving and everyday it got better than the day before.

All I knew for sure was that I wanted my daughter to have the best life that I could give her. And just when I thought things were finally settling down, before I knew it, I went from adjusting to being a single parent to now fighting in court for custody of my daughter two years later. This was another battle I faced. I remember the moment when I received the court papers. I felt defeated, betrayed, hurt, and full of rage. I completely lost it that night. I could not believe what was happening. The very thing that was keeping me alive was now being threatened to be taken from me. One of the things I remember the most from that night is that my mother and my then boyfriend, now husband, couldn't do anything that night but watch me. The love I had for my children is indescribable, unconditional and unmatching. To think of losing her was unimaginable to me. Here I was once again having to fight, not only to prove myself to the court system but to prove to myself that I would come out of this in one piece. Everything was at stake- my peace, my sanity and my being. That night it was me and God. Here we were again, God and I. Me with unanswered questions on top of pain, disappointment, hurt, anger, unforgiveness and there was God waiting for me to give it all to Him and let Him handle it. That night there was a battle between me, myself and I. The former "me" who wanted to go all the way left and take matters into my own hands, "myself" who was paralyzed because she couldn't fathom that she was ever in a battle like this to begin with, and "I" who knew there was greater in this and that it wasn't about her, but it was about how God would get the glory out of this.

That night, I drank an entire bottle of Patron straight. It was literally a fight inside of me but the "I" won. The treasure of God inside of me won the battle. In the midst of it all I heard a voice that said, "Get up daughter, you have to fight. The battle has already been won but you need the training." So I got up the next day, and went to war. I held on to the word of the Lord so tightly because it was literally the only thing that would get me through. That was the last time I took a drink throughout the entire battle. All I needed was the Word of God. My now husband, who was my boyfriend at the time, was so supportive during that ordeal. He allowed me the time I needed to get myself together. One night as I was praying, I heard God say, "in order for you to be with the man you are with and one day have a family with, you have to forgive." That was an extremely hard concept to accept. To be honest, I was not trying to forgive but everyday I realized I needed to. It didn't happen right away though.

~Love Always Wins~

After 2 years of constant war in family court, the petition for mediation was finally granted. The crazy thing about all of this was although I was going through all of this, I still had to smile and act normal because I was raising a little girl and I didn't want her to be affected by this crazy. While all hell breaking loose in my life, I still put my makeup on, got dressed and tackled life with a smile. I am not saying that I should have been in bed, but pretending to be okay wasn't good either.

Throughout this process I was able to see who my true friends were as well. In the beginning everyone is around to "watch" if you will get through or how you will get through what you're going through. The sad truth is that most people don't care about what you're going through. They care enough to want to know but not enough to do anything about it. When I got that, I stopped going to friends in hopes that they could save me, only God could do that. The calls and texts stopped coming and they were on to the next piece of "drama". People barely knew what I was going through, all I knew was that I had to keep moving.

At this point I had spent over $10,000 in lawyer fees and started going to church more again to develop a deeper relationship with the Lord so I was more equipped to go through this ordeal. In addition I was in counseling with my Pastor as well. It was a very lonely time in my life because although I was in the crowd no one really saw me. Looking back, God is so awesome because He sent me sergeants, lieutenants, and battle buddies to train me and see me through. One of the wisest women I know, Dr. Rev. Lashley, gave me a great piece of advice that would change the trajectory of my life. She said that it takes two people to compete on the dance floor and there can't be a dance competition with only one person. With that I decided to get off the dance floor.

We were coming down to the last court date and we had our last meditation session. The final decision would come down to whatever came out of this mediation. Here I was sitting across the table from a man I once loved, a man who I was going to marry, a man I decided to have my first child with, a man that although I was so angry with, I could only feel compassion for because he was a man who was hurting just like I was. As I sat there filled with rage, I heard a familiar voice say, "its time to forgive. Tell him you love him for the precious gift of a daughter that he helped you to have." Before I knew it, I said, "I love you, you know. I am not in love with you anymore but I'll always have love for you because without you she wouldn't be here." I could not believe what I had said. He started to shout across the room and the mediator asked him if he heard what I told him. He proceeded to argue but the mediator interrupted him again and said, "I don't think you heard what she said." In that moment the creature from the blue lagoon that was in a fit of rage and anger sitting across the room took a breath and came back to the man I once knew.

I'm not saying that things got better in that instant and we were best friends after that because that would be the farthest thing from the truth. What I will tell you is that we NEVER fought like that ever again. Eventually we came to a mutual respect for each other and I owe it all to God. Even when I felt alone and misunderstood He knew exactly how to help me.

Position Principle: Be consistent. Stand firm and lean on God. Stay in the race no matter what. Understand that pain births champions. It's in the consistency that you see results.

~PRAYER FOR ENDURANCE~

Father God,

In the name of Jesus. I come to you right now humbly yet boldly before your throne of grace. Father, my life is wearing me down. I'm tired, exhausted, working very hard and running in all different directions. I know there has to be a change. I don't have enough time but I don't know any other way to be God. I know you have a plan for my life and your word says it's a plan to prosper me to give me hope and a future (Jeremiah 29:11) so I surrender to your will for my life. Help me to adjust, tell me what you want me to know about your plans and what I'm supposed to do and how I can move out of my own way. Teach me Lord, how to persevere in the midst of a storm. Make me ready to receive, renew my energy, give me strength where I'm weak, send me fresh wind and air into my being. Give me a restored spirit and motivation to make adjustments when and where needed. Forgive me Father, because I have allowed the enemy to convince me not to come to you with this, I have allowed the enemy to persuade me into giving up time and time again and for that Father, I am truly sorry. I have overestimated my situation and underestimated your strength. In a moment of confusion and exhaustion, my perception, which was altered and my distance from you left a big gap for the enemy to come through. God,

I believe you are my provider, my helper, and my healer. I believe you have empowered me to take hold of those things that keep me in bondage. So Lord allow me to see, so all that is in front of me is released so I can be able to go forth and do your will. I rebuked the spirit of heaviness and brokenness off of my life and I asked you to give me a clean spirit so I can approach every issue with a good and positive heart. Father, show me something I have not considered. I'm not attached to my own way, my family's way or the world's way. I declare and decree as a new creature in Christ, I am committed to put my life and right order with you. So help me to tune in to you every morning for divine instruction on how to be better, how to move in the midst of the storm, how to endure life and where it's taken me. Father, I believe that there's more for me from the depths of my heart, so keep me grounded. God moves people and places and things off my agenda that don't line up with your will for my life. I release the spirit of feeling overwhelmed and I give it to you and I take responsibility for my actions and decisions. From this day forth, I will show up decently and in order. I declare and decree that I'm coming out victorious. Allow me to persevere. I believe because it is written. Blessed is the man who perseveres under trial because when he has stood the test, he will receive the crown of life that God has promised to those who love him. I believe that I have the victory in Christ and I will create a plan and move forward with you, God as the head. I believe you will give me the practical steps to make the moves that are unnecessary so I can have more. My strength is being renewed even now.

In Jesus Name we pray,

Amen.

For anything that becomes visible is light. Therefore it says, "Awake, O sleeper, and arise from the dead, and Christ will shine on you."

~ Ephesians 5:14

Phase 3: LABOR

~THE AWAKENING~

~CHAPTER 6~

PREPARATION IS KEY!

Blessed are those who find wisdom, those who gain understanding, for she is more profitable than silver and yields better returns than gold. "
~ Proverbs 3:13-14

The next phase in the birthing process is the Labor phase. This process can honestly last as long as it needs to because nothing comes before its time. When you go into labor, you may initially experience a time of uncertainty and self doubt. What feels like contractions may, in fact, be simply preparation trials. Anticipation and excitement are mixed with anxiety, and perhaps with some fear about what to expect. The problem is identifying this stage. Looking back on my life, I have realized that this phase lasted a very long time because I struggled to take responsibility for where I was in my life. Labor really started when I began to understand the meaning of obedience. That was another hard concept to wrap my head around. After many trials and tribulations that I encountered over the years, I was forced to wave the white flag and surrender. In labor your body doesn't do what you want it to, if it did it wouldn't be the scariest part of the process. A woman is literally never as close to death as she is when she is in labor. My back was against the wall, everything I did fell apart. I literally felt like I was losing my mind. My health was failing, my bank account was at zero, my family was broken and all I could do was look up.

I learned to look at life a little differently. I really wanted different for myself, I wanted more and I would not get it living the way I was living. I hated who I was becoming and so I really started my search for more. I was living from a place of hurt and pain which caused me to rebel which led me to become disobedient. I was literally having spiritual abortions by not living in my full potential and that was killing me. There is only a certain amount of times a person's body can handle surgery before the body gives up on them.

Are your body and mind failing you? Are you burdened with the weight of life? Do you feel like you are carrying the weight of the world on your shoulders? You might even be at the point where you are saying that's not your problem because you are obedient, responsible, and doing what you are supposed to. Here is the thing, I was there too but did you know the world's way of being obedient is not God's way. Is He calling you to let go of some things, do something you've never done, or go in a different direction? Did you know partial obedience is still disobedience.

I was exhausted, mentally, emotionally, physically and spiritually. I got tired of doing things my way because it wasn't working. The fact is, it never worked. I had gotten to the point where all I could do was look up and raise the white flag. I had enough of trying to do life my way. It was my endgame. There was no big epiphany for me, it was straight forward. I realized that I couldn't do this by myself. I had to surrender, I had to go back to the one who created me, the one who had put purpose in me, the one who gave me these gifts and talents and that was when the real journey of my life began.

~Yes~

As much as I thought just saying "Yes" to God was going to solve my problems, I had to realize it wasn't going to be that easy. I had to go back and pick up the pieces where I had been broken. I wasn't prepared to give birth, and I knew it. I had to prepare mentally, physically and spiritually for what would soon be the fight of my life. I had to face myself in many ways. It began with me taking responsibility for my actions and thoughts. I had to realize that I was the only person who owed me anything, it wasn't about what my dad did. It wasn't about what my mom didn't do. It wasn't about what happened to me or what didn't happen to me. It's about what I learned from what I went through. It was about the lessons I would take away from the things that I went through. It was about me, and how I was going to course correct all of the things that didn't go well in my life to get to where I wanted to be in my life. Funny enough my mother would always tell me that life did not revolve around me (another one of her famous Mama B quotes). I could not stand it when she said it, of course I didn't even believe her because it didn't make sense to me. Back then I thought it was all about me but I soon realized she was actually right, life actually did not revolve around me. I just existed in life and if I wanted to be a relevant piece of it, I would have to stand for something more.

I had to realize quickly that I was not in control because God was. He just gives us free will but His will always trumps ours. So in order to course correct I had to allow the preparation process to take place. It was the only way I would be ready for more. Preparation comes in many forms and cleaning up my messes was one of them. I had to ask myself some tough questions and even worse I had to be able to handle my responses. So if you're ready, ask yourself, "what are the things that you need to do in order to take responsibility for yourself, for your thinking, and for your actions?" Strangely enough, I have learned that the key to freedom is Obedience.

~Levels~

In order to take responsibility for yourself there has to be a level of obedience and humility that comes with it. That revelation was probably one of the hardest relizations I have ever had to face. The meaning of obedience is to be in compliance with another's law or to follow one's authority. That was a very hard concept to understand for a while. I first had to understand what it meant to be responsible which is being accountable or having a duty to deal with something or someone. Being responsible means that you are in a place where you are able to make decisions independently or without authorization. To go a little deeper it also means having control over or for someone or something but it does not mean while you don't need permission that you're not under someone's authority. You still need to be in alignment with those in authority. Basically, whatever you think or do is not only in direct correlation to you but to others as well. Life is relative in every aspect, what you and I do affect others in some way. After realizing that concept, I realized my life was off kilter because of me. I did not function in authority and I made decisions selfishly, never realizing that my decisions affected others. My decisions affected those I was responsible for and that maybe the case for you as well. After seeking clarity and understanding in this area, I soon found that authority and control were my problems as they might be yours as well. I wanted to be in control of my life, therefore I had a hard time respecting authority and submitting.

I soon learned that the authority that was put over my life, whether I agreed or not, was for a reason and that I had to obey, not because I necessarily wanted to but because I am supposed to. There is a mandate in my life from God and I believe He makes no mistakes. The ones He put in authority over me would be the ones to help me fulfill the purpose He put inside of me for His glory, not my own. With that in mind, understand that there is hard work involved in you birthing out your possibility.

~The Process~

If you are reading this book, there is a mandate on your life for better, there is MORE. There is greatness inside of you waiting to come out. The world needs what you have and it's your job to serve them. I think that sometimes we get so caught up in not wanting to listen to the people that were put as authority figures in our life because of what they've either done to us or what they did or did not do in their own lives. But in fact there is a purpose for whatever they have done or did not do. After realization and repentance in the preparation process, there is a level of humility and understanding next. I had to humble myself and understand that it wasn't about me agreeing with the person who was in authority over me, but understanding that whatever they were telling me to do or not to do was about building me up instead of tearing me down in one area or another. Now what I am about to say might be harsh but here is the truth.

Whatever you have gone through, whatever you may be going through is preparation for your greatness, your win, your future, and you. No matter how bad or how sad, you have to believe it is happening or happened for your good. So, my Dad calling me out of my name happened for my good. Being betrayed by friends happened for my good. Having a child out of wedlock happened for my good. All of the "bad" things that happened to me were for my good. Those life events showed me who I was not and who I actually was. When I look back on my life, I am stronger than I would have ever thought. The question remains "is authority a bad thing, and can it be used to oppress?" I say it's not bad when you know the person's motives and intentions. Is it coming from God? Know that everything God does is out of love even when it might look harsh. So if the person in authority is coming from a place of love and peace accept that their authority although it may seem harsh at times.

This is why it is important to know God's will in your life. He can use a bad situation and work it out in your favor. So yes, my mother and I didn't agree with a lot of things, but where was she coming from? She was in a place of authority but she was always coming from a place of love. At the end of the day, she really just wanted me to be better and sometimes we need to understand and see that to get to the next level. Not everyone is against you. Rejection causes us to think everyone is against you and that is not actually the case. You don't have to agree with those who are in authority over you, but you do have to respect them and you have to respect yourselves in your decisions as well.

~ Careless~

Understanding that you were made for more and in order to get more, you have to be teachable which means you have to be able to listen. I know because I definitely did not listen pertaining to wellness and self care. But it was through my disobedience that helped to birth mybusiness. I had to suffer first to understand the importance of taking care of myself. I had an autoimmune disease, leaky gut, depression, low adrenals, migraines, hair loss, weight loss and other health issues for years before I realized I was hurting myself by giving of myself to everyone else but myself. I think it's absurd that we give ourselves to everyone else but yet we tend to neglect ourselves. When we fail to prepare ourselves in mind, body, soul and spirit in essence we are actually preparing for failure in those areas.

Mind, body and spirit preparation is about self-care and wellness. Our hygiene practices, etiquette practices, attitudes, and our health and nutrition practices are apart of it as well. Not being prepped in these areas actually hindered me throughout my life more than I realized.

~What Are You Saying?~

As a little girl, many people said that I had an attitude and I would always get upset that they said that. But the fact of the matter was, I did have an attitude. We all have attitudes actually. The question is what kind of attitude did I have vs. what kind of attitude I should have had? What they were really trying to say was that my attitude was negative and to be honest, that was true. What I didn't understand was that because I had such a negative attitude, I was attracting negativity because of my attitude. I had to learn that you don't have to agree with everyone, and you also don't have to be fake with your feelings but you can be pleasant in your attitude. Your attitude determines what you receive in life. It determines where you go and what you get in life. If you give off negativity, you're only going to attract negativity. But if you give off a positive attitude, you're going to attract positivity. It's a proven fact. Your attitude works very simply, it's energy. Your attitude is your presence and it precedes you, it goes before you. Having the right attitude prepares you for the right blessing.

Take a moment to look at how you show up in your life. Ask yourself how many times you probably entered a room with a nasty attitude, can see how that might have affected the outcome of situations. Your life is a lot to do with your attitude. One of the things I learned in this stage was to start how you want to finish. I am not saying that everyday is going to be a good day, but you have to decide on how you want your day to go. How you show up will determine how you end. Most people don't realize that your attitude is a part of your self-care routine as well. Having the right attitude sets up your day. It's ok to speak to your mindset and tell yourself how you want to show up. When you wake up on purpose you set the temperature for the day. Showing up with a beat face, a bomb outfit, and a stink attitude is not cool.

Going a little deeper, let's talk about your hygiene and etiquette practices. This might get a personal here but I promise you I am leading into a point. How often are you bathing? Do you have a dental routine? How often do you go to the doctor? When was your last check-up? These are things that we need to do in order to prepare us for another level but oftentimes these are the things we neglect until it's too late. Before you know it you will be having more aches and pains than you can remember. Take care of yourselves now while you still can. Take time for yourselves while you still can. You're never too young or too old to make yourself a priority. You might be thinking etiquette is a thing of the past but let me be clear, we need it more now than ever before, especially when you want people to respect you enough to listen to you. Etiquette is a set of practices that allow you to interact with others without overstepping boundaries. Some of which are simple such as common manners like saying, "please and thank you".

With the entrance of social media, which is an uncharted territory in etiquette. Being mindful when texting, calling, face-timing and posting someone. Set boundaries for yourself and respect others boundaries as well. Following proper etiquette practices will allow doors to open for you and not knowing them will have doors shut in your face. Respecting a person in every aspect starts with respecting yourself first. How you treat others and yourself is the standard of how you will be treated. Knowing there is a place and time for everything is key. How you present yourself through your attire is very key in preparing you for your future. I am not saying women are to only wear dresses but dress how you want to be approached.

~What Are You Doing?~

Another area I wish I was prepared for was how food would affect my body. Nutritional values are not only to be a discipline, they need to be instilled in us as a way of life. Everything that looks good and tastes good is not good for us and everything that looks bad and sometimes tastes bad may actually be more beneficial. We are what we eat after all. A lot of my gut issues came from what I ate or did not eat as a child, especially as a teenager and as a young adult. The truth is autoimmune diseases like hypothyroidism, depression and others are partially connected to nutrition. Basically I wasn't eating right. My stomach lining was messed up badly from eating and not eating on time. The effects didn't happen right away but by the time I did start to see the effects, it was too late. By the time I looked at myself, I wasn't even there. I had to learn to make time for myself and not feel guilty about it. I don't live to eat, I eat to live. I make sure what I put into my body is going to benefit me. Is it going to be purposeful? Is it going to restore me? What are the benefits? What are you eating? Whether you are a young girl or an older woman reading this book, know that you are important and what you eat is important. The reality is, we will not be young forever. Everything we do or not do takes a toll on your body. What we do in our teens affects who we become in our twenties, thirties, forties, fifties and so on.

Take your life more seriously by paying more attention to your body. Not only to the foods that we eat, but what we listen to, what we watch and the company we keep. Even our conversations are a very important part of what we put in our body. It's a part of your self care. When people talk negatively, it doesn't help you to be positive. We have to be very mindful about what is around us and what goes in us. Wellness is something that I don't think we put as much emphasis on as we should, especially when we're growing up. We pay more attention to the destination of growing up rather than understand it's a journey and we need to take time to get to that destination. There is a level and another aspect of your wellness or self care that is rarely spoken about as well. It's your perspective, your spirit care, your belief system. We all have a story and we see and receive things differently but in every storm you can still be grateful? What does being thankful look like for you? What are you grateful for? I believe in God, the Father, the Son and the Holy spirit. Everything I do is in correlation with what He wants for me. It took a long time for me to say that and stand in it. But once I did, life started to align similar to labor pains.

~It's Time~

Once everything is in place, then your water breaks and you know it's time. Labor tends to bring things into perspective. It removes doubt and replaces it with what is. I could have looked that all life has dealt me and stayed in a victim position but instead I chose to see things differently and take on a victor's mentality. The point is you owe yourself. What are you doing for you? My health took multiple hits during my life because my perspective wasn't clear. There were days when I was so drained, I could literally feel my blood sugar drop. I wake up almost every morning in pain but no matter what I still give thanks and praise to God. I honestly thank Him because it could have been worse. Again, I was giving so much of myself to everyone else, I now had this affliction to remind me that if it's not for Him, then it doesn't matter. I I was pouring out but wasn't pouring back into me. Wellness is about obeying God's word for your life.

⁓The Real Issue⁓

Suffering from depression is definitely a serious issue. Let me state that once I started on this journey, and got saved I have NOT suffered from depression. Now I am not saying that I have never had a bout of sadness because I have, but it has not lasted more than a couple of days. Now that I am prepared in that area now, I now know how to handle it when it comes. To be honest, most of the time it's because I'm trying to do things out of my strength. If we know we are being stressed from work for example, we then know we need to do things to help fill us back up which can be taking supplements, vitamins, healthy foods, exercise and most of all, rest. Everyone is different and I am no doctor but I am speaking from my personal expertise with battling not only mental issues but a thyroid condition and physical ailments. I have come through all by the grace of God.

When my health was basically compromised because my body was fighting itself, it was because I ignored the signs until my body literally shut down on me. It was at that point I learned how to level out, balance out. I had to learn how to listen to my body and know when it has had enough.

In the era I grew up, all I knew was hustle and grind. There was something most of us don't know and it's called rest. It was given by God. While sleep is always a good thing, I am referring to resting in God. Rest comes in many forms like change of environment, stopping for a moment and sitting with God, breathing and meditation but most importantly praying. There is grace in the grind if you do it God's way. We're always on the go for our own agenda that doesn't obey God. We are not listening to Him because we can't be still long enough to hear Him. Ultimately God is the absolute authority and we must surrender and give everything to Him. Listen to what He has to tell us so that we can take care and do the things that He told us to do.

~Declare It~

In the Labor phase we talk to ourselves to get through the pain and we have to do the same spiritually. Declaring and speaking wellness in every area of your body, mind, soul and spirit is very important. It is one of the most important things that I can stress. As a woman of God, it's definitely a pillar in the wellness chapter of our lives. What are you doing on a day to day basis to renew your spirit? Are you praying? Prayer changes everything. The one thing I did not know growing up was the power of prayer. Prayer can shift an atmosphere. It might not change things when you want it, but it definitely changes things when it's supposed to change. Prayer helps you, it guides you. It's the best therapy I've ever had. Being alone with God and just giving Him your thoughts, giving Him the things that hurt you, the things that make you angry and waiting for him to speak a prayer is so amazing. You can pray about everything and anything. And the greatest thing about prayer is that it doesn't have to be a specific time or place or way to pray. There are the long drawn out prayers and then there are the get to the point prayers. Either way, prayer is just simply talking to God. I remember when I first began a prayer life, I was so afraid to pray because I thought that I needed big words. I used to even sometimes try to memorize what I wanted to say. My Pastor would always tell me to just let it flow, let go of control and relinquish my heart to God and He will allow the words to flow. It didn't happen right away because of my control issues but eventually it flowed. What a release!

God just reminded me, come to me with all of it. I'm not looking for the big words, I'm just looking for you! I just want your heart. I want your full attention. That was it! From the day I gave God my full attention when I prayed, and allowed the words to flow out of me it was honestly a spirit to spirit connection. I want to implore you, reading this now to surrender to God, give Him all that you have and watch Him work. Trust

Him. He will come to your rescue as you pray. At the end of the day, God knows it all, we don't have to come to Him pretending to know it all. We just need to come to Him and obey His word for our lives. Obey what He's trying to teach us. Make wellness a staple in your life because it is actually preparing you for success, and for where it is that you truly want to be. The best preparation for tomorrow is doing your best today. Taking time to take care of your mental, emotional, physical and nutritional well-being will lead you into what God has for you. He is preparing you for more. Your body takes nine months to prepare to give birth. Your body has to be strong enough to be able to carry that child for nine months and so it is in the spirit. You have to be able to carry the purpose that God has given you. He will wait until the right time to birth out the possibilities of that purpose. In order to have the life that you truly want, you have to prepare your mind, body, spirit, and soul for more willingly.

Position Principle: Put on your armor! The key to maintaining momentum in this fight for our lives is to stay ready so you won't have to get ready. Put on your helmet of Salvation, the breastplate of Righteousness, gird your waist with the belt of Truth, put on the Gospel Shoes of Readiness and pick up the sword of Truth (The Word) and the shield of Faith and get ready for war! Trials and tribulations are the preparation we must go through to get to our greatness.

~PRAYER FOR PREPARATION~

Dear God,

Forgive me for complaining. Forgive me for not being obedient to the process. Forgive me for thinking that my way is better. Father, I recognize that I need you. I need your cleansing, your forgiveness and your guidance. I need your presence and your love. I need your mercy and compassion. Give me a fresh start, making me whole and pure so I can come into your presence and be in fellowship with you. Lord, I thank you that You have armed with strength for the battle; you have subdued under me those who rose against me. You have also given me the necks of my enemies, so that I destroyed those who hated me (2 Samuel 22:40-41). Lord, may your strength be perfect in weakness (2 Corinthians 12:9). I pray that your power would rest on me and prepare me for the battle that is in front of me. You are my strength, you are my healer and you are my provider. I lack nothing because I have you and I rely on you to help me stand strong in the midst of the storm that I am facing right now. Blessed be the Lord my rock, who trains my hands for war, and my fingers to battle- my loving kindness and my fortress, my hightower and my deliverer, my shield and the One in whom I take refuge, who subdues my people under me (Psalm 144:1-2). May your praise ever be on my lips. As I rejoice in you, in your mercy and grace, in your forgiveness and love, fill my mouth with praise for you. May my words point the world back to you as I remember your perfect faithfulness, your love, your provisions. Prepare me for this season, a season that represents more about you and your plans for me than goodness. Prepare me to find peace in the midst of this chaotic world, to set aside the craziness of this life for the beauty of your love. Help me to make sense out of my circumstances. Help me to see a way out of no way. Draw me into your presence so I can sit, soak, enjoy every moment of knowing I am secure in you. Thank you for this season of preparation. I will no longer ask why me? Instead I will say thank you because you chose me.

In Jesus name I pray,

Amen

"For the weapons of our warfare are not carnal but mighty in God for pulling down strongholds…"

~ 2 Corinthians 10:4

~CHAPTER 7~

THE FIGHT FOR YOUR LIFE!

For where your Treasure is, there is your Heart also.
~ Matthew 6:21

Eventually there comes a time in labor when you must work hard and become focused. The contractions become very strong as the cervix opens for the baby to be born. Each contraction stops you in the midst of whatever you are is doing and demands your attention. You need a lot of support and encouragement at this time. You may also want relief from the pain and struggle. You are no longer able to maintain full awareness of what is going on around you. At this point you might turn inward at this time, and cope with each contraction quietly, within themselves. This is what I call "The Wrestle." It is the time when you begin to wrestle with yourself and then with God.

I started to wrestle with myself because I was trying to figure out who I was. Was I what I pretended to be me? Was I who "they" said I was? Or was I who God says I am. After sitting with myself, I was able to gain clarity on the fact that although I was reading my Bible, I did not believe what I was reading. I had reached a stage where I felt like I was being broken down and stripped away. The only thing left with little choice was to go with the process and to trust its outcome. Although I was passionate about my next level, it felt like death, in this experience. At this point I could only trust that the experience was a call to a different and deeper union with God, a call to allow myself to be gradually converted and transformed. The pain and struggle calls us to trust that something will come to birth, and that God has not completely abandoned us. I started to ask the question "who am I?"

~An Invitation~

If we're honest with ourselves, we all have some sort of insecurity. What I had to realize is that insecurity is an invitation from God to escape the danger of false beliefs about who we are and find true peace in who He is. We are invited to enter more deeply into a true relationship with God. Excluding God from our lives does not allow us to fully live and by admitting God into our lives we enlarge and enrich our lives and have more. The call to be a Christian is not a call to suffer as such, but rather to enter into our suffering in the knowledge that it leads to conversion and transformation. It provides a place to birth new life and hope of deeper union with God and essentially freedom.

"So let's not get tired of doing what is good. At just the right time we will reap a harvest of blessing if we don't give up."~Galatians 6:9

The question of who I was plagued me for a very long time so I started to search for the answers. I searched in the wrong places at times but I don't regret it because I can say I know for sure who I am and whose I am now. The definition of identity is who you are, the way you think about yourself, the way you are viewed by the world and the characteristics that define you. Now for me, I started with my name. As they say your name is the easiest way to identify you. So I looked up Nadia, and it means hope. This is when I had my first aha moment. I then defined the word hope, which meant a feeling of trust. Why did I have to trust anyone or even myself? What I came to realize was that I didn't need to trust myself but to trust God in who He says I was.

~ Citizens of the Kingdom~

Through extensive research I realized that not only was I not of this world, but that I was a citizen of the kingdom of heaven. For some reason it all made sense. Feeling as if I didn't belong, now made me feel connected to something bigger. It gave me a sense of peace within. I am a treasured daughter of God. Knowing that brought me such a fulfillment that I now wanted to be who I was supposed to be. Finding my identity was one thing but establishing my identity was another. This phase of labor is a painful and a seemingly unending process.

When you are in labor, you tend to move from one position to another. One day you're good and the next you're not. Basically your choices, decisions and being are all over the place. This is called confused identity, where you are trying to do and please everyone but God. So here I was again, knowing who I was but not feeling comfortable enough to be it. It's a struggle because to some degree your will and God's will are fighting against each other. There is no relief from the pains which come with increasing frequency and intensity. He will make you uncomfortable in the most comfortable positions until you surrender to who He says you are. At this point you can either wrestle against this force, or relinquish control to it. That is the calling of our true identity and it is found when we stop trying to be who we "think" we are and start becoming who we were created to be. This is the battle between self will and God's will.

First and foremost your identity is established in a foundation of the Word. Knowing where you actually come from makes a difference. You are the treasured daughter of the Kingdom, which means your father, is God. So with God being your father, you have abundant potential to be whoever you want to be. You can do ALL things through His son, Jesus Christ. There is no limit to the possibility of potential that you have inside of you . But here is the catch, you have to believe who you are to

Him. I searched the Bible and scripture after scripture told me who I was. As I read those scriptures, I felt the holes that no one could see being sealed up. I was being made whole. My confidence, my self-esteem, my character, my integrity, my intentions and my motives were being rearranged for good because now I had found my purpose in Him. They were once thwarted and rooted in my pride and ego because I was trying to control everything but I was learning to trust in Him and slowly relinquish control. It was a process but it was worth it. Do you know who you are? Here are some reminders if you do and if you don't here are some answers.

- We are created in His image~ Genesis 1:27
- Before we were born He set us apart~ Jeremiah 1:5, Ephesians 1:4
- We are adopted into His family~ John 1:12, Ephesians 1:5; 1 John 3:1-2
- Our lives have purpose in Him~ Ephesians 2:10; Acts 17:28
- In Him we live free from condemnation~ Romans 8:1
- We are wonderfully made~ Psalm 139:14

When I look back, I realize that I made all of those dumb decisions because I didn't know who I was. On a late night in my bathroom as I stood in my shower I broke down in tears just thinking about how not knowing who I was led me down a road that could have killed me. I couldn't stop crying. I asked God to forgive me because I didn't know and now that I did know, I would do better with my life. That night as I was sleeping I was awakened by a voice again. All I heard was, "treasured." I knew the Holy Spirit was speaking to me and it was time for me to get my life. I didn't sleep that night, I stayed up writing in my journal and cross referencing my Bible and the dictionary to define the word treasured. It would take me years before I could fully discover not only the meaning of the Word in every aspect of my life. As I started to discover the treasure, I soon realized it was God in me.

Position Principle: Your identity can only be found in Jesus Christ. Don't allow anyone to tell you who you are. You are chosen. You are called. You are loved. You are blessed. You are forgiven. You are beautiful. You are special. You were created with a purpose. You are lovely. You are cared for. You are strong. You are important. You are a new creation. You are protected. You are empowered. You are family and you are His.

~PRAYER FOR IDENTITY~

Dear God,

I humbly come before your throne of grace to say thank you. Thank you Jesus, that because I have received you, I am a child of God. Thank you that you have paid the price for me to be cleansed from all sin. Thank you that you sit at the right hand of the Father and intercede for me because I believe in you and have received your spirit into my heart. Thank you that I am now a joint heir with you of all that our heavenly father has for his children. Thank you for giving me authority to pray in your name and to know that you hear my prayers according to your will and your time. Help me to always have a clear conscience before you, let there be nothing in me that gives the enemy a reason to think he has any kind of invitation to undermine what you are doing in my life. Help me not to give into fleshly desires and enable me to be as Holy as you are Holy for I know and it's only by your spirit working in me that this happens. I understand that Holy doesn't mean I am perfect but that I live a life in devotion to God. Trying my best to live by and within His standards for my life. Help me to keep my mind focused on serving you. I know I was redeemed for something far more precious than gold and that and that is the blood of your son. Help me to live in a manner worthy of that. Lord, help me to be the person that you've called me to be. God, teach me to understand the authority you have given to me, especially in prayer. Enable me to use that authority to break down strongholds the enemy would attempt to erect in my life and in the lives of others whom you put on my heart. Keep me from doubt that I am qualified because only you supply me with everything I need. I take my orders from you and no other. I have authority because I have you. Lord, help me to be okay with separating myself from anything or anyone that is not holy in your eyes. Teach me to be separate from anything that is not glorifying to you. Teach me to stand in liberty, which you have freed me. I do not want to live below your standards for my life. Show me anything and anyone in which I need to separate myself. Thank you for completing the work you have begun in me. Show me where I have pride so I can repent of it. Teach me how to take care of myself for I know it is your desire for me to be whole. Show me where I displease you, help me to know the right things to do and convict me when I don't do them. Enable me to always walk led by your spirit so that the fruit of your spirit is produced in me. Father, remind me daily that my identity lies in you. Fill me with a fresh flow of your love, joy, peace, patience, goodness, faithfulness, gentleness and self-control. Help me to stop thinking about what I am not and instead focus on what I can be. Help me to not worry over what I should be focused on what you say I am. I will not conform to this world, but I will be transformed by the renewing of my mind so that I may prove what is good and acceptable and the perfect will of God.

In the name of Jesus, Amen.

So if the Son sets
you free, you will be
free indeed.
~John 8:36

Phase 4: Delivery

~PUSH & PRAY~

~CHAPTER 8~

THE RELEASE

Fear not, for I am with you; be not dismayed, for I am your God; I will strengthen you, I will help you, I will uphold you with my righteous hand. .
~ Isaiah 41:10

In order to discern whether you are ready to birth in the spirit or in the natural, there has to be an act of letting go. In the natural this time of transition usually occurs just before your cervix is fully dilated and you are at the end of the hard and painful part of labor. You may begin to make some involuntary grunting or pushing noises; however you are not at the end yet. Although birth is near, it is not yet clear when you will push the baby out and what type of delivery it will be. Everything hangs in the balance. The final push hasn't happened yet, and even when you don't think you have anything left, you still have little strength left to cope with the next contraction. In the spirit this requires patience in the midst of the excitement;

it may mean that we experience restlessness and discomfort in our lives as we wait vigilantly to see what will happen. Feel the feeling but don't become the emotion. Witness it. Allow it and release it.

This is a time of surrender, in both the physical and spiritual lives. Very much like when a close relationship ends or someone important to us dies. We no longer have any control, and we may feel that a part of us is dying or has died. We may feel that we want to give up, or that we do not know what to do with ourselves any more. God may seem distant but know He is near. It is imperative that you must release some things before you are actually able to give birth. There must be an acceptance within yourself for this release to occur. It means actually letting go and letting God. There needs to be an act of submission to God that has to happen. This sounds great but it doesn't feel great. Even after all that I went through, there was still a very huge piece of me that still wanted to be in control. I was actually trying to control what and how God was moving in my life. I remember after church I would feel so empowered and feel as if I could conquer the world but by Monday, I was a total mess again. I had slipped up and found myself begging God for forgiveness. As much as I knew there was more for me, I also felt stuck and trapped. Similar to when a woman is in labor and dilation stops for some reason. It's a place of uncertainty. All you can do is pray and give it to God or abort the whole process and end up harming yourself or the baby.

"So let's not get tired of doing what is good. At just the right time we will reap a harvest of blessing if we don't give up."-Galatians 6:9

~Let Go and Let God~

Holding onto offenses can kill you and your birthing. In order for God to move in my life the way He wanted to I had no choice but to let go. I had to forgive everyone who had ever wronged me but most importantly I had to forgive myself. I finally went to speak with my father and if you know Caribbean parents, it is not the easiest thing to do. They are not communicators so this was hard for me but I knew I had to do it. Before I knew it, I was in tears, I basically asked him to forgive me for being so upset with him all these years. I apologized to him because I didn't want to carry any baggage, I finally understood what happened all those years ago. I wanted to be free to become the woman God was calling me to be and so I had to realize that he was the best father he could be and for that, I am grateful. Ultimately, my true Father is in Heaven and as my earthly father, he could only give me what he could and that is what he did. I cried because I was free. You see I don't understand why he raised us in the way he did but that doesn't matter but I do understand why God allowed it.

It's amazing how things like unforgiveness, bitterness, anger, rejection, and abandonment have the ability to hold us hostage and basically force us to abort our purpose. I made a decision that I was no longer going to abort God's will for my life so I had to let EVERYTHING that was holding me down had to go. Now, I'm not saying it was that easy because it wasn't. God was working on me for a while but it did come down to a simple decision, what did I want? And so I will ask you, what do you really want? Do you want a life of peace or a life of turmoil? Offense can literally make you blind if you let it. So many of us go through our lives blind to our real purpose of being here and some of us even die with our purpose still inside of us because we couldn't see what was really important.

Now, my father and I are no besties, but there is a mutual level of understanding and respect that I couldn't be more happy for and that's only because of the grace of God. After we spoke, I went home and made a list of the people I needed to forgive and prayed about whether I should reach out to them or make peace within my heart and let it go. But from that day forward I vowed that I would never allow anyone to take up space in my heart. Now, I am not saying it's easy because it isn't but I try my best not to hold any offense. I am learning everyday not to put my expectations in another human being but in God himself.

~It's Brewing~

Changing my way of thinking helped me to be fully prepared to give birth to what God was brewing inside of me. In order for God to move freely in our lives we must relinquish all control to Him. A few years ago, I was sitting in my office and I heard the Lord say, "shut it down." I thought it was my mind playing tricks on me so I paid it no mind. A couple of weeks after that I ended up going to the doctor and found out I was pregnant with my son. Since I had just had a miscarriage my doctor told me that I would have to take be on bedrest. Immediately I started to freak out because as an entrepreneur , you can't just call out. She looked at me and asked me if I wanted this baby or not. That night I came home and got on my knees. I did not know what to do. I want to say that it was easy to let go but it wasn't. It was actually one of the hardest decisions I've ever had to make in my life. I cried everyday about it until one afternoon I went outside to move my car and I literally fell in the middle of the street. As I layed on the ground, I heard "SHUT IT DOWN, NOW!" A car to my right screeched and a guy got out and helped me up. All I could do in the moment was thank God. I went to get checked out and as I got out of the hospital, I immediately shut EVERYTHING down. I was obedient to the audible voice of God. I had to make some very hard decisions but I eventually took my hands off my baby (my business) and gave it back to God, the one who gave me the vision for it in the first place. This was the first time in my life that I had absolutely no control and although it was scary, it felt good. I felt free. What I realized is that we actually have no control anyway and that's where the stress comes from. We think we do. I did not know what God was going to do so I had to learn to trust Him.

There is a level of acceptance a woman has to go through when she is in the process of delivering her child and the same in the spirit when you are about to give birth to your purpose. Although all hell is breaking loose, you have a sense of peace that is unexplainable. Around the same time that I was dealing with closing down the business I went to a women's shut in prayer service in Pomona, New York which was two hours away from where I lived. My sister in Christ drove me because I couldn't drive. I took my mom and my daughter. My husband and I were the only ones who knew that I was pregnant at the time. There were stations set up for prayer, meditation, journaling, studying and reflecting when we got there. Attendees basically moved throughout the stations from 10pm-5am.

As it began, I had to run to the bathroom and I realized I was bleeding. I immediately got scared but I did not tell anyone. The bleeding got heavier every time I went to the bathroom. I did not know what to do. All I could do was pray. The last station I went to was the journaling/writing station. I couldn't even write at first, all I could do was cry. I did not understand what was happening because I was constantly bleeding. Finally, I got myself together to write. At first I started off angry with God but then I made peace with Him and His will. I was begging for my unborn child. I felt like Hannah, if I could begin to imagine what she felt when she prayed to have kids.

Part of my letter read,

"Please Lord, let this pain in my womb be you multiplying my baby instead of expelling it. Father God in heaven, whoever is praying against me and my baby, I pray you deal with them in your own way. I pray for their souls. Father, I pray you will keep me whether I lose this baby or not. Keep my husband and daughter. Father, I believe you are saving my baby and me right now. I am so thankful that you have not forgotten me. Your words said that today has enough problems for today and tomorrow already has enough to worry about, so I will not worry, I will trust in you..."

In that prayer and at that point, I accepted whatever God's will for my life. There was no more fight in me to fight God. I accepted it was going to be whatever it was and that I was going to be just fine because I knew God was in it. I let go and let God. Throughout the entire session I was still going to the bathroom and I was bleeding heavily but I gave it to God. There was an unexplainable peace inside of me. I know, I was basically having a miscarriage but yet I was at peace. I honestly didn't even think of going to the emergency room because I knew God was in charge.

In the midst of the Bishop, Jacqueline E. McCullough saying announcements, she immediately turned in my direction and said, "Someone lay hands on the woman in the pink! The enemy will not snactch another baby from her womb!". The next thirty seconds felt like 30 minutes. Before I knew it my Pastor who was sitting directly in front of me facing me jumped so high she almost touched the ceiling. My mother who was behind me let out a sharp scream and was holding her stomach, and my friend was sitting right next to me and fell to the floor while screaming. Before I knew it, I had so many hands praying over me. After they prayed, the Bishop said, "My daughter, the Lord said it is done, in Jesus Name." On our way home, my mother told me she felt her womb do a backflip and my friend said she actually saw a hand and then she saw a light knock the hand out of the way. I kept looking at the color of my sweatsuit because I was still in complete shock. When I got home and told my husband, he couldn't even comprehend what happened.

Position Principle: Accept that God has you in the palm of His hand and that He will never drop you. Trust in Him always, even when it doesn't make sense, when you're scared and even when you think you know best.

~PRAYER FOR TRUST~

Father God,

I enter your throne of grace boldly, yet humbly with confidence given to me by your son, Jesus Christ. Father God, you are Jehovah, the great I am, the beginning and the end. You are El Shaddai, the God of much more, Jehovah Shalom, the Lord my peace, Jehovah Jireh, the Lord my provider. There is none greater or higher than your name. I confess that sometimes I forget how great you are. I confessed that I try to pick up and deal with things on my own. Forgetting that you are my provider, father God, I confess that I want to put all my trust in you but it's hard. I have been disappointed so many times and it hurt so bad. Lord, help my unbelief, help me to not expect from man but only from you. Remind me that you are not like a man and trusting you is the safest thing I can do and be. Your word says that you have commanded me not to be discouraged or afraid because you will be with me wherever I go. You are the sovereign Lord. Your covenant is trustworthy and you have promised only good things to your servant. Father God, You said that those who know your name, trust in you and you will never forsake those who seek you. I seek you now, Lord and forever. I trust in your unfailing love and my heart rejoices in your salvation. Some trust in temporal things like people, things and even money, but I am making a declaration that I am trusting in your name, the name of Jesus, the Lord, my God. I say, you are my God and I will trust in you, when I'm afraid I will put my trust in you. When I am worried, I will put my trust in you. When I am lost, I will put my trust in you. You are the Lord almighty, blessed is the one who trusts in you. So I declare and decree that I am blessed because I trust in you. I am no fool Lord. Your word says that those who trust themselves are fools, but those who walk in wisdom are kept safe. So Father, I thank you for keeping me safe. I thank you that I will not lean on my own understanding in every area of my life, but that I will submit all my ways to you. Lord God, you will make all my paths straight and I will trust in you, Lord, with all my heart. I thank you, Father, that no weapon that shall ever form against me will prosper. And every tongue that rises up against me shall be silenced. I thank you, Father, that no principalities, no witches, warlocks, strongholds, demons or anything sent by the enemy can touch God's anointed, but with the authority given to me by your son Jesus Christ, will prosper. I will rise up against every mountain blocking or distract or distracting me from the purpose in which you have created me in the name of Jesus. I pray for your will over every area of my life, and I know for certain that you have covered every single area of my life so I don't ever need to worry. I will trust in you and not in my own ways.

In Jesus' name, Amen.

Have I not commanded you?
Be strong and of good courage;
do not be afraid, nor be
dismayed, for the Lord your God
is with you wherever you go."

~ Joshua 1:9

~CHAPTER 9~

THE BIRTHING

Therefore, my beloved brothers, be steadfast, immovable, always abounding in the work of the Lord, knowing that your labor is not in vain in the Lord . ~1 Corinthians 15:58

Pushing a baby out is hard work. The pain is different; the contractions are strong. In this phase the baby is actually coming. Now you are able to work with your body to give birth. Not only can you feel it but there is a "knowing" as well. But you need encouragement as well. Your painful cries turn into deeper grunting and straining efforts. Your body has completely surrendered to this experience, and all you can do is go along with it. You might be feeling as though you are going to split apart, which makes you not want to push for fear of what is on the other side. There is a tension between what your body is naturally doing, your pain, and the fear that her body will be significantly harmed.

In our spiritual processes, too, the pain and struggle of transition is difficult as well. Eventually it gives way as the new life of faith comes to birth. Pain is still there, but it has changed; there is now direction for it. New life is in sight, excitement is evident, and what seemed like endless pain and confusion has now turned into hope and change. Although here may be a tension between bringing the new life of faith and fearing what may happen next when this occurs. Don't be afraid of the experience. You may feel overwhelmed, and uncertain whether you can birth the new life that you are called to bring forth but believe you can. If God brings you to it, He will bring you through it.

~ The Discovery~

Six month after the experience at the Shut In, I gave birth to a beautiful healthy baby boy who brought me to another level with God. I can't help but praise the Lord! He actually heard me and for that I owe Him my life once again. I know that it was only after I accepted Him, asked for forgiveness and let Him have control over the situation that He saved my baby. Acceptance can only happen when you fully release control back to God and then blessing begins to flow. Eventually, I got the word from the Lord, that I could reopen my business and this time around it ran even better than the first time and our profits increased as well.

Birthing your purpose is not an easy task and most of us are still struggling to and that's the purpose of this book. Many women are walking around having miscarrages and spiritual abortions and they don't even know it. I know because I was one. I walked around accidentally, feeling lost and confused. We have been conditioned and taught to live by the world's standards and not the kingdom's and so we end up living in confusion and beneath our potential. It stops now. I believe there has been a mandate in my life to teach Kingdom daughters that there is MORE for our lives. We all were born with a purpose inside of us that is unique to us. There is no need for competition, envy or jealousy because what is mine is mine and what is yours is yours. The Lord orders ALL of our footsteps.

As Treasured Daughters of the Kingdom, our purpose is not for us, it's for God's Kingdom. God uses our gifts and talents to develop us into our purpose to bring His Kingdom on earth. It starts first by discovering that we have a purpose, then to birth it, and then to walk in it. Birthing purpose gives your life meaning, it improves your self-perception, it gives you a firm foundation and it sets you apart from others. Our identities and our purpose is only found in Jesus Christ. This is the foundation we need first in order to move forward towards true freedom. True freedom is the ability to glorify God by becoming who He wants us to be. Walking in the plan and purpose He has for our lives. To be successful in every area in life, you must acknowledge and accept that there is a reason you are here on this earth and that reason must be fulfilled in order to satisfy God's plan for your life. To walk in your purpose you must understand the ultimate purpose as a Christian and also the unique purpose God gave you.

~The Beginning~

Now my journey started way before I thought it started. Becoming an entrepreneur was not easy because it was a calling from God. It helped me to birth my purpose and stretched me in many ways. It started with my love of hair. My mom used to help out a friend often who owned a salon and we went there every weekend. I saw women come in with slouched shoulders, sad eyes and sorrowful demeanors and leave standing tall and feeling confident, and beautiful. I also saw women in their sorrowful state be kind and then after their transformation turn into mean spirited women as well. Now I am not saying every woman was like that but that stood out to me. After college I decided to go to cosmetology school and I came across many women who were hurting in one way or another. They came to the beauty salon in search of help to beautify themselves on the outside which was good but it didn't satisfy their needs on the inside. I wanted to do more, I wanted to give them hope so that they become more than they were. Although I loved hair, I loved the women's spirit more.

I will never forget a lady who came into one of the salons I was working at. She wanted a total makeover. As I started to cut her hair she began to cry, and when I asked her what was wrong, she said it was because I was cutting off all of her beauty. I immediately stopped, spun her chair around and spoke directly to her spirit. I asked her why she felt that way and she responded by saying that her hair was the most beautiful part of her. Her hair was long but it was breaking really badly much like her spirit. We talked more and I explained to her what true beauty is. It is the peace and love that you have for yourself that actually radiates from the inside out, it is the spirit of God. I told her she was a Treasured Beauty, a woman who radiates the spirit of God within. She just had work on believing that she was treasured by God. We talked as I styled, we cried and we laughed. When she left she gave me a huge hug and a $100 tip. It wasn't even about the money for me but more about the smile she left with. That was when I knew it was so much more than the money and even the hair.

For me it was about the transformation of the women who sat in my chair. Whenever I told my colleagues how I felt, they told me I was crazy. The industry had changed a lot in the last couple of years. Healthy hair was not something that was promoted often. I believed healthy you, healthy hair. Deep down I knew there was more and this was only a piece of it. I ended up going into salon management for a little bit because I thought I was in the wrong profession but God knew the reason. I ended up building my dream space where faith and beauty could coexist and The Treasured Beauty Hair Lounge was born.

~In The Middle~

After a few years of opening my salon, my daughter began to itch her arms and legs till she bled. Her doctors were telling me to just give her the steroids they prescribed because at the time they thought she had eczema but that did not sit right with me. The side effects of the medication they prescribed were worse than the problem itself. I sat at the top of the stairs, one day while I held my daughter and called my aunt who is a pharmacist. I didn't know what to do, she had swollen up so so badly she looked like she was filled with water. My gut wasn't settled and I wasn't going to make a move unless I knew it was the right decision for her. She had already been through a lot. Her mere existence was a testimony. She came out thriving as a completely healthy baby girl in every way when the doctors said it wasn't possible. That day we both sat there alone and cried, while I figured out what to do. In the midst of my tears I heard a calm voice say, "take a picture of it and search for it on the computer." I got up, wiped my face and took a picture and went to the internet. I sat there and searched for hours, trying to match every rash picture that was on the internet to hers.

Finally, I found one, it was Elizabeth Haselback from the VIEW at the time. She said hers was caused by gluten and there it was, the answer. I called the doctor back and told him I wanted to test her for the gluten allergy. I started to cry again because I finally found the answer to our sleepless nights filled with waking up to blood everywhere from her scratching her skin until it bled. I knew immediately that I had found the answer because there was a release in my stomach and I just knew it was God. We found out after the tests that she did have a gluten sensitivity allergy and therefore we had to remove ALL gluten from her diet.

Gluten is a natural ingredient that comes from wheat and used very commonly as a preservative in most processed or packaged food, most our bodies are not able to handle the amount that is being used in foods lately and so it produces inflammation which causes a reaction to the skin and the brain.

~Alignment~

Being raised with old school caribbean, I had a different plan to attack this gluten issue. I decided to attack it from the root with herbs. It's easier to put a bandaid on things rather than deal with the root. Unfortunately we do the same thing with matters of the hurt as well, which doesn't help us to give birth.

None of this happened overnight, mostly everyone thought I was crazy for my approach to this but it just felt right. Unbeknownst to me, my life was starting to come into alignment with God's will. Through extensive research, trial and error I created a healing skin salve under the function of the Holy Ghost. I attacked the issue internally with natural supplements and externally with natural ingredients for complete healing.

After seeing the wonderful results on my daughter's skin, I just knew that I could not keep it to myself. I could only imagine the amount of children suffering not to mention their mothers suffering with them. I eventually packaged and introduced the Delicate salve to the world and that is how my second business, a skincare company, Treasured Beauty was born. I didn't understand what God was doing but I knew He wanted me to use my gifts to heal. Treasured Beauty was created to heal, transform and connect. It was a combination of prayer that encouraged and the healing of natural ingredients that provided a different experience to skincare. But this new journey took a leap of faith. Creating a skincare company based on healing through aromatherapy was uncharted not to mention it was one of those things that was supposed to be something small but God had another plan. Honestly the first few years were actually very difficult. It was scary because I had no real direction back then. I had to rely on God. There was no google university or the College of YouTube. Although I went to college for Business Management, no amount of college classes would prepare me for real entrepreneurship. All I had was the fact that I heard God say "Treasured." I was tired physically, mentally and emotionally and I think God knew it.

~The Rebirth~

I was in a place where I was not being valued and definitely not treated worthy of all I was giving because I was still using my gifts for other things. I had a second encounter in my sleep again and this time I knew it was God. I was awakened in the middle of the night by the Holy Spirit once again. All I heard was "are you ready?" It was a deep yet subtle voice, asking, "Are you ready?" After the third time I finally said, "Yes." The voice then replied, "Are you ready to use the gifts I gave you for my kingdom?" I nearly fell off the bed. In that moment it was so clear, I was using the gifts and talents given me by God to fulfill His purpose for my life on futile things. I immediately started to cry. I felt so badly, I was not using the gifts God gave me in the right way. I felt so bad. All I could do at that point was ask God to forgive me. I decided at that point to move forward with the Treasured Empire, where faith and beauty can survive. Even though I was scared, I was going to take a leap of faith and introduce a faith based empire to the world. I was being reborn as a new creation.

"For behold, I create new heavens and a new earth;
And the former shall not be remembered or come to
mind". ~Isaiah 65:17

I decided from that day that everything I did would be for Him. No longer would I let the rules of the world govern how I lived my life or even how I did business. God was officially going to be the C.E.O of not only the company but of my entire life. By no means was this an easy task, but it is worth it every day. To have a level of peace within is priceless. A peace that the world didn't give me so the world couldn't take it away.

~My Purpose~

That was the best decision I have ever made in my life. But things definitely got harder rather than easier but I was at peace and that's all that mattered. Throughout my journey I realized that my purpose was to teach women how to uncover the treasure of God within themselves. I finally gave birth to my purpose and there are endless possibilities to who and what I can be with God's grace and that is my desire for you as well. I am not done becoming the woman God has called me to be but I am also not the woman I used to be. God is not finished with me yet, it's just the beginning. What I know for sure is that the process of giving birth is long, hard and tedious. It takes strategy, insight, principles and lots of prayer. It takes skill to learn how to navigate through life and wisdom to know how to position yourself for the next level. There is more in each one of us and for every one of us.

We can think of pregnancy as a symbol of waiting and watching time, during which our secret hopes and dreams develop. A time of discernment, while listening and waiting for something to be revealed. In the last phase of labor, we desire encouragement and support through the struggles of the spiritual journey, and in transition we must trust that our desperation, anger and weariness will bring forth the birth of a new life in the Spirit. Birth is a time of joy and celebration, along with relief and awe at the gift of God's grace and love in our lives. And finally, there is the postnatal period, when we combine this new life of faith, and move forward. I hope this book helps you understand the phases of the spiritual birthing process. Keep in mind that everyone's journey is not the same but with prayer and the Word of God you have everything you need to embrace the next chapter of your life and get into position to birth your purpose. The next few chapters are postnatal strategies that helped me to continually navigate my journey after birth and I know it will help you as well.

MORE is not a destination but a place of understanding within Yourself and accepting God's will for the next steps of your life.

Position Principle: Stop fighting and accept your assignment! There are unlimited possibilities in birthing your purpose. You were destined to do and be more than you can ever imagine.

~PRAYER FOR PURPOSE~

Father God in Heaven,

I come to you boldly yet humbly in adoration of who you are. Lord, You are a great God, who could have chosen anyone but you chose me. You created me in your image and likeness. You have set me apart and created me to be unique for your glory. Help me to be okay with being original and not to duplicate others around me. Help me to see the gifts and talents you have given me to share with this world. Help me to understand that my purpose here on earth is to use my gifts and my talents for your Kingdom. Father, I ask for your forgiveness for looking for my purpose in everything else but you. Forgive me for using my gifts and talents for everyone else but you. Forgive me for seeing them as common. Thank you for the ability to look within to find my purpose in all aspects of my life. You do nothing by accident and I thank you for creating me on purpose. Allow me to embrace my differences, my authenticity, my faults and my truths. God, I have realized that the answer is not in searching for my purpose but living a purposeful life in everything I do. Perhaps we have it all wrong Lord. Instead of searching for our purpose, we should be searching for you and along the way our purpose will manifest itself in and through us. Help me to see that. I need your help in shutting off the voices that don't speak the truth. Bring back to the moments where I can hear you clearly. Give me clarity and insight on my next moves. Show me my part in your plans. I resolve trying to figure it out on my own. Allow me to accomplish your purpose for me without me having to fully understand. Grant me the courage to walk in my own shoes, at my own pace, especially when the journey is lonely. Keep my eyes focused on my purpose in You. Help me to fall in love daily with your will for my life and with exactly whom You created me to be more each day. Increase my faith in you and myself. Allow my faith to become bigger than my faith. God, continue to remind me that faith is a gift from You and not a result of my efforts. I will no longer focus on things I cannot do. I will walk in the assurance of what I know I can do through You.

In Jesus name, Amen.

Therefore, if anyone is in Christ,
he is a new creation.
The old has passed away;
behold, the new has come.

~2 Corinthians 5:17

~CHAPTER 10~

THE REALIGNMENT

The Lord will open up his good treasury, the heavens,
to give rain to your land in its season and to bless all
the work of your hands. And you shall lend to many
nations, but you shall not borrow.
~Deuteronomy 28:12

Most people discuss the birthing process from conception to delivery and stop but I think it's important to know that the process doesn't just end there, it's actually just beginning. The recovery stage is actually just as important as conception. Anyone who has actually gone through real birth knows that it's just as important to to learn how to breast-feed or feed the baby as it is to maintain a healthy diet to actually birth a healthy baby. The same goes for us who now have a new life in Christ. After we birth our purpose, we must learn how to nurture and keep it healthy as well. This requires patience and time, allowing it to grow and develop in its own gradual way. Nurturing may take many forms- silent, contemplative prayer, reflective thoughts, rest and care for ourselves spiritually, wise counsel who holds us accountable. I believe having the right people in our circle is key during before and after this process. Every Christian woman needs an Elizabeth, a person who God has given the right vision to see what you are birthing. A person who can be your spiritual nurse or midwife to help you birth it out and help you to nurse it after birth.

> *"As iron sharpens iron, So a man sharpens the countenance of his friend."~Proverbs 27:17*

~After Care~

Birth is over and there is a new world that opens up for you as a mother as you begin to learn how to care for your baby. There are routines and schedules that need to be established. You might experience considerable pain and discomfort for some time after the delivery. You may experience 'after-birth pains' when you are breast-feeding, as your uterus contracts back to a smaller size. It is also common, about three to five days after birth, for you to feel sorrowful and emotionally down, as a result of the hormonal changes that are occurring. This can turn into postpartum depression in which I had as well with my first child but not with my second and I really believe it was because I had an understanding of the process. The same goes for a spiritual baby- your purpose. The after birth process requires not only adjusting but awareness and discernment. This is also a phase of recognition for everyone involved. After any deep experience of transformation, there must be a repositioning of the mind. There is an act of getting into alignment with our sense of self, of others and of God in our everyday living. You might find it difficult to readjust to the world, as you emerge into a new life as I did. In both the physical after giving birth, you are never the same again.

> *We cannot solve our problems with the same*
> *thinking we used when we created them.*
> *~Albert Einstein*

~Who's Next to You?~

It is very important to stay grounded and stand firm in who you are and whose you are. I am so grateful to God as I was not only granted some amazing Elizabeth-like friends who believed not only in me but what I was carrying. Also, spirit filled women of God, who provided me with wisdom, knowledge and understanding. Without them being my spiritual midwives I don't know where I would be. I call them my "Heavenly Holy Ghost Filled Hitters," they play no games. These ladies have delivered me, tarried with me, told me the truth even when it hurts but most of all they prayed with me and for me. I am forever indebted to them and God.

They saw who I was supposed to be even when I couldn't see it. They had faith in me when I lost faith in myself. They are led not by their emotions but by the Holy Spirit. I am forever grateful and humbled to know these powerful women of God. I am forever changed by not only my encounter with these women but more importantly my encounter with the triune God, the Father, the Son, the Holy Spirit. So when someone says, she has changed, my response is, yes I did! I was made for more and now I know it. I will never ever again play small or settle for less than I deserve. It took me a while but I got it. Although God had more for me, I couldn't receive it until I was ready mentaly and then I had to get into position.

~The Gift~

I used to think abundant favor, the blessings of God and the peace that surpasses understanding is for a special type of people but throughout my journey I have realized that it is available to those who want it. Because of the undeserving favor God has shown me in my life, my prayer is that every woman who reads this book receives the same thing I did so I created the The Intentional Plan-Strategic Steps to Positioning Yourself for M.O.R.E. In the next few chapters, I will give you the strategies and tools to help you *Maintain* a healthy mindset so you can *Overcome* negativity in order to *Reposition* yourself- Mind, Body & Spirit so you can *Experience* God's best for your life.

Whether you are new to the idea of the spiritual birthing process, feeling stuck in a phase or feel lost and confused as to what to do now, this is the plan for you. No matter what phase you are in know this- God has already equipped you with what you need to be able to live a life of greatness. Jesus was born great and when He died He gave us the gift of greatness through the Holy Spirit. Victory is ours and the battle has already been won. Each principle has steps and if applied correctly they can lead you into becoming a woman of Godly purpose and help you to maintain the freedom that God has been given to you. This plan is a go to guide to help you position yourself the right way for God to move not only in you but through you. These next steps are not for the faint and weary. It's for those who are tired of living everyday beneath who they were designed to be. So, if you're ready let's get to work!

Position Principle: Stand up, dust yourself off and stop playing small.
There is greatness inside of you! Stop dimming your light. Come into the light and be who you were designed to be. Be great and spread the gospel, not for you but for the one who made it possible for you.

~A PRAYER FOR MORE~

Father God,

I humbly come before your throne of grace thanking and praising you for your continuous blessings and prosperity upon my life and upon the lives of my family.

I thank you for being the Alpha and Omega, the beginning, and the end. Father, you are the most high God. No matter the situation I can call on you. You are, Elohim, the God of creation. You are Jehovah, the great I am. You are Jehovah Shalom, the Lord my peace, the peace that passes all understanding. You are my peace in the midst of confusion, chaos, trials and tribulations. You are my peace in every stone of the law of my life. You are Jehovah Nissi, the Lord my banner. You are my victor and you give me victory over sin, sickness, poverty, and over every enemy of my life. You are El Shaddai, the God of much more. I thank you God that you provide more than enough for me, more than my needs, more than any area of lack in my life. I thank you that I have favor in all things. God, thank you that you bless me exceedingly abundantly and above all I can ask or think. According to your word, you said that you desire above all things that I might prosper and be in good health even as my soul prospers.

Father, when I think of where I could be, or what I was, I have to look towards the heavens and say thank you. You are always there for me. I don't deserve your love but yet you give it to me anyway. I can't help but to say thank you, although that will never be enough. Father, I know that you called me for more and although I do not know what all the time, I know you will never leave me nor forsake me. You are the same yesterday, today and forever. You are Jehovah's Sabul with the Lord of hosts. You have assigned strong, mighty and warning angels over my life. You have given them charge over me to keep me in all my ways. You deserve all the praise. You Lord, are my shepherd. Because of you, I shall not want or be in lack of any good or needful thing. You lead me, you guide me and you watch over me in all of my ways. God, I thank you for being the God that shows me that more is attainable. Thank you for the many blessings that you have given me, and more that are to come. Lord, help me to stay in your will. Help me to clothe myself in humility so that I will never forget where my blessings come from. I will remember you Lord my God, for it is You who gives me power to get wealth, and that You will stay faithful to Your promise that You swore to your fathers, as it is this day.

Help me to glorify you in all that I do and in everything I have. Father, your word says that the blessings of the Lord makes one rich and he adds no sorrow in it, so I pray that the enemy cannot rob or steal from me or my family. Help me Lord to be good stewards over all you've given. Give us guidance and teach us the way. Teach me the way you want so that in doing so, I can rebuke the enemy who comes to steal

what I have. Father, I am so grateful for all you provide--
the knowledge, wisdom and understanding. Father God, I
am thankful for so much more than just the riches of the
world but the riches of the spirit-peace, love, kindness, joy
and goodness. More than anything I am thankful that I can
be a servant. Thank you for teaching me how to give without
receiving anything in return. Father, you said, give and it
will be given unto you: good measure, pressed down, shaken
together and running over will be put into your bosom. For
with the same measure that you use it, it will be measured
back to you. Allow me to be a generous person to give in a
way that pleases you. Help me to trust you and not in money
or riches. Help me to always be ready and willing to share.
Help me to store up a good foundation for the time to come.
Teach me to be wise and everything that you give me. Thank
you that you have provided God, the more that I could, I
could never ask for. The more that I just know that is your
will for my life. God, thank you for preparing me. Thank
you for setting the table for me. Thank you for helping me to
see that it is not about the trials and tribulations, or even the
storm, but the discovery of You in it all including me. That
is the greatest treasure of all. God, I will lift you up and even
now, I continue to just reference your name. Father, there are
familiar spirits that have been in my family and I am declaring today that it is stopping with me. There's not going to be
another generation, this is it. The buck stops here. So Father

I rebuke all strongholds, occult practices, and all the things that came against your will and your way for our lives in the name of Jesus. For me and my house we will serve You Lord. I walk with you, Father, I will talk with you Father, and I will continue to put you forward and call you Lord.

In Jesus Name, Amen

Phase 5: RECOVERY

THE MAINTENANCE PLAN

Strategic Steps to Positioning Yourself for M.O.R.E.

~CHAPTER 11~

MAINTAIN

This section of this book contains the actual steps I use to stay focused after giving birth to my purpose so I could continue to live a life of more. It is straightforward and I believe it is very beneficial for all of us as we continue to move forward in the life God has intended for us. I pray that this section of the book will be a light and a guide to you in preparation and maintaining for you to not only give birth but continue to position you for a life of more for the Kingdom.

PRINCIPLE #1: MAINTAINING A HEALTHY MINDSET

Take Back Control

Set your minds on things above, not on earthly things. ~Colossians 3:2

This step is the most important one out of all. It is the most in depth because it is key to everything else. Everything begins in the mind. From the beginning of the Bible, time and time again we have seen how words infiltrate the mind and shape our thoughts and actions. Our mind determines the daily choices and decisions that impact our present and future. There needs to be a more intensive and intentional approach to what we allow into our minds daily. Here is an exercise to help you with this. Draw two columns on a piece of paper and take a moment and reflect on all the things that were either said to you verbally or you saw growing up. Write down the things you saw and heard in the first column. In the second column write down what your beliefs, morals, and values are today (be honest). Now connect the things you saw and heard to who you are today.

Do you see how the things that you saw and heard as a child have changed your perspective. Take a moment and sit with it. Now I want you to write on the top of the paper, the words Bye Bye Little _____ and write your name in the blank. What you are doing is saying goodbye to that little girl who was tainted by the views of the world she saw. Now rip that paper up. You will no longer allow that little girl's perspective to guide your life. Tell her it's okay and that you love her but she has to go now.

It's time for you to take back control over your mind. In Ephesians 6:12, the Bible states that *"For our struggle is not against flesh and blood, but against the rulers, against the authorities, against the powers of this dark world and against the spiritual forces of evil in the heavenly realms."* This clearly means that there is a war going on whether we see it or not and in 2 Corinthians 10: 4-5 it states *"For though we walk in the flesh, we are not waging war according to the flesh. For the weapons of our warfare are not of the flesh but have divine power to destroy strongholds."* Basically what these two scriptures tell us is that we are engaged in war, whether we want to acknowledge it or not. We have an enemy and the battlefield is in our minds.

Phillippians 4:8, tells us that *"whatever is true, whatever is honorable, whatever is just, whatever is pure, whatever is lovely, whatever is commendable, if there is any excellence, if there is anything worthy of praise, think about these things."* In other words, think about things that are positive and bring you joy. Can you see how our mindset is distorted from early in our lives? Some might not believe in "the devil" or " an enemy" but I believe that there is an opposing force and you can call him whatever you like. What we do know is that it's against us. Our view and our hearing can hinder us in many ways to the point that we can be our worst enemy. Once we establish that, only then we take back our control. It's actually very simple in theory but a bit hard to do consistently. We need to pay very close attention to what is flowing into our minds through different avenues like what we listen to, what we watch, what we see and what we say. We also have to understand that there are two minds. The mind of the flesh and the mind of the Spirit. We need to establish who's talking. Know that none of us are perfect and sometimes the voice of our flesh can get louder than the Spirit but don't give in. There is power in taking a thought hostage and rebuking it in the name of Jesus.

When a thought arises you don't have to receive it. Stay encouraged, stay positive, and no matter what, believe in the Word of God concerning your life. You have to live your life on the overflow. Meditate on God's word day and night, and decide to be transformed from what you were to something new in Christ. Pay attention to the words you speak over yourself and those you love because words are powerful, they influence how you think and see things.

Death and life are in the power of our tongues, and those who loveit will eat its fruit. ~Proverbs 18:21

Set Conditions for Your Mind

For those who live according to the flesh set their minds on the things of the flesh, but those who live according to the Spirit set their minds on the things of the Spirit. For to set the mind on the flesh is death, but to set the mind on the Spirit is life and peace. For the mind that is set on the flesh is hostile to God, for it does not submit to God's law; indeed, it cannot. Those who are in the flesh cannot please God. ~ Romans 8:5

Setting the conditions of your mind is the next step. Before you can set the condition first you need to access the actual condition. Is it peaceful and calm, is it anxious and worried or is it sad and cumbersome? Are you a double-minded and two-faced, are you pretentious and fake or are you transparent and real? Don't feel bad because I have been all of these at one time in my life. Here is the thing, you can change all of that by deciding today, right now that you no longer want your mind but the mind of Jesus. Yep, it's that simple. In Hebrews 12:2, it states *"Do not be conformed to this world, but be transformed by the renewal of your mind, that by testing you may discern what is the will of God, what is good and acceptable and perfect."* Decide right now that you are no longer going to live by your rules and standards for your life. I know some people might argue and say it's not that simple but I believe it is. I will say the continuous walk in this direction is not easy but the initial yes is. It's making one sharp turn in the direction of Jesus and everything else will follow.

The problem is that we play on the edge too often and we end up hurting ourselves. It's one decision in the right direction that will make your life that much easier, even in the midst of the storm. But before we completely go there, let's recognize the elephant in the room or should I say the Spirit in the room. If you didn't know, the Holy Spirit is a gentleman, He doesn't force His way, He waits until He is invited and He does not stay where He is unwanted nor does He stay where there is confusion. So making the decision to set the condition of our minds also is making the decision to make room for the Holy Spirit in our lives. The Holy Spirit and the flesh mind cannot dwell in the same space because one will eventually take over.

However the Holy Spirit can coexist with your spiritual mind which is always ready to yield to the Holy Spirit at any time. Even a spiritual mind has to be trained because the fleshly mind is always there. Our minds are prone to wander so we have to discipline ourselves and our minds to stay fixed on Jesus. We have a propensity to reason with ourselves, to feel like we deserve and that leads us astray all the time. That's why it's very important to be a doer of the Word and not just a reader because if you don't you'll just be fooling yourself. You have to decide to trust God with your mind because there are two thoughts that can tear down the whole thing- doubt and unbelief. Doubt is a choice and unbelief is disobedience. This is where faith comes in. Do you have to see it in order to believe it? " *Now faith is the substance of things hoped for, the evidence of things not seen".* -Hebrews 11:1 which means that faith is the evidence of the things we don't see at the moment. Access the conditions of your mind and take a real deep look inside yourself. Decide what condition can you truly live your best life with.

Adopt a Growth Mindset

For God is not a God of confusion but of peace. -1 *Corinthians 14:33*

155

Now that you have learned how to make smart decisions to choose right thoughts, the final step in this process is to adopt a different mindset. Some call it growth and some call it the mind of Christ, which means a new heart and spirit. Your mindset governs how you make choices and handle decisions. Your mindset can also alter your perspective. You can choose to hold onto things or it can choose to keep things. The Isrealites spent forty years in the wilderness because they had a fixed mindset. The ultimate key to having the mind of Christ or a growth mindset which keeps us looking forward and propels us into our greatness by believing there's more. It prepares us to give birth to our purpose in a healthy way. A fixed mindset hurts us and hinders our progress because with this mindset you focus on is behind you instead of moving forward.

Let's delve right into it so you can see why you need to ditch the fixed mindset. A fixed mindset has many different voices. Voice 1 says, "my future is determined by my past." Voice 2 says, "I can't! It's too hard and I don't want to take responsibility, so do it for me." Voice 3 says, "It's always my fault." Voice 4 says, "I don't deserve God's blessings, I'm not worthy." Voice 5 says, "Why can't I feel sorry for myself, my life is trash anyway." These are just some of the thoughts a person with a fixed mindset has. What keeps you thinking this way is your vision. You operate in life with a tainted vision and that's why you can't seem to see better. You are focused on yourself but if you look up for a moment, you would be able to see a whole new world.

Now I am not saying it is easy but again it's a decision and a prayer. We can't do anything on our own but through prayer we can do all things. Ask God to reveal yourself to you. To show you how you operate through tinted lenses.

Ask God to identify the problem and most times you will see it's you. You can change the way you look at things by being thankful from the smallest detail around you to the biggest. Have an attitude of gratitude. Keep your eyes looking up and I guarantee you that you will develop the mind of Christ. Focus on healing, teaching and serving and before you know it you will be living like Jesus. It doesn't mean life won't get hard because it will but because of your new perspective, you will be able to get through it. So make a choice everyday to grow, to show up and make each day better than the last and I promise you before you know it, your mind will shift into a position of dominion and authority.

~CONFESSIONS FOR THE MIND~

- I set my mind on things that are above, not on things that are on earth. (Colassians 3:2)

- I will not conform to this world, but I will be transformed by the renewal of my mind, that by testing I may discern what is the will of God, what is good and acceptable and perfect. (Romans 12:2)

- I will not live according to my flesh and I will not set my mind on the things of the flesh, but I will live according to the Spirit setting my mind on the things of the Spirit. To focus my mind on the flesh is death, but to focus the mind on the Spirit is life and peace. (Romans 8 : 5-6)

- I will think of things that are true, honorable, just, pure, lovely, commendable, and if there is any excellence, if there is anything worthy of praise, think about these things. (Philippians 4:8)

- I will not be anxious about anything, but in everything by prayer and supplication with thanksgiving I will let my requests be made known to God. And the peace of God, which surpasses all understanding, will guard my heart and my mind in Christ Jesus. (Philipians 4:6-7)

- My son, if you receive my words and treasure up my commandments with you, making your ear attentive to wisdom and inclining your heart to understanding; yes, if you call out for insight and raise your voice for understanding, if you seek it like silver and search for it as for hidden treasures, then you will understand the fear of the Lord and find the knowledge of God. (Proverbs 2:1-5)

- You keep me in perfect peace whose mind stayed on you, because he trusts in you. (Isaiah 26:3)

~CHAPTER 12~

OVERCOME

T his principle is contingent on one thing, belief. *The LORD is my light and my salvation— whom shall I fear? The LORD is the stronghold of my life— of whom shall I be afraid? ~Psalm 27:1* You must believe that there is more for you and life does not have to be this way. That will be your saving grace like the rescue tube when someone is drowning. You have to believe with every being in your body for you to come out of this. Being a person who suffered from mental issues for many years, I can tell you it is work but it will ultimately be your belief that keeps you afloat. Some days will be harder than others but you can fight this. You can make it through. Again, I am no doctor but the following are some actionable steps I put together to help you through. I believe mental issues are a twofold process and there is not a one solution fits all. I would advise seeing your doctor and getting a complete physical exam done because most mental illness stems from lack of minerals that your body needs to survive.

Most of us try to cover up the issue with a Band-Aid (medication) before we actually find the source of the problem, and attack it there first. That actually makes it worse because now you have allowed the roots to go deeper. I would then suggest seeking the right spiritual counseling. I say the right counseling because not everyone is equipped to handle mental issues. Also brace yourself because in order to free yourself from this there are some harsh truths that have to be told. So being that I am not an expert in this area I can only provide simple steps for maintenance. If you need help please speak to a professional. But know that you are an overcomer because Jesus already overcame the world. In John 16:33, it states *"Theses things I have spoken to you, that in Me you may have peace. In the world you will have tribulation: but be of good cheer, I have overcome the world."*

PRINCIPLE #2~OVERCOMING NEGATIVITY

Overcoming negativity daily can be achieved by doing the following things:

Use Your Words

Words have power. Be careful how you use them. Speak positivity over yourself and those around you. Prayer is essential, it is a powerful tool. Pray about everything. Pray without ceasing.

Through prayer you will find the words to speak over yourself. There is something so special about rising early and going into your secret place -where you and the Lord meet. Putting on your spiritual armor so you can tackle the day.

Consume Wellness

Wellness consists of a few things as we discussed in the earlier chapters. Spirit care and self care are a part of a healthy wellness lifestyle. Eating well is another vital step in the process. Making sure we consume the right foods at the right time is essential. Resting is also key. Not only do our bodies speak to us but so does God. Sometimes He needs you to stop so He can talk to you. Journaling is also very good as well. Exercising is also necessary in whatever form. It is imperative because in order to handle the magnitude of your purpose you need to be strong both mentally and physically. Laughter is also a part of a good wellness regimen. It's good to laugh at yourself, life has enough drama you don't have to be it as well. Lastly, have fun, try to incorporate doing something fun for at least 30 minutes a day.

Watch Where You are Standing

Pay attention to who is around you. Not everyone one who is in your circle is for you. Don't listen to what people say, watch what they do. You can't change people but you can change people. At the end of the day we only have control over ourselves so why not look at ourselves. Where are you standing? Are you standing in circles that don't serve who you are trying to become? Are you standing in muddy waters where everything is about how bad life is? This is important because for some reason we find ourselves in places that we don't belong in or next to people who don't have our best interests at heart. We often find ourselves in comfortable situations and that can stifle us and cause us to feel negative. The places we tend to stand also have energy and if you're a person trying to stay in a positive space you cannot be in places where the energy is negative. This does something to us and before we know it we start feeling "off." Be mindful of where you are standing and who you are standing next to. It matters, energy transfers. Negative feelings come from negative thoughts and negative thoughts come from negative energies. We already know who rules the air so to go a little further ask yourself what kind of energy are you giving off?

Speak Up

Confess over yourself using scripture and declarations. This is not a binding ritual practice but as a guideline and framework to launch you into the practice of speaking up for yourself to yourself. As you speak out these confessions,

declarations and affirmations ask the Holy Spirit to guide your words, thoughts and faith as you make your way to more. I understand that every person reading this is unique, and only you know what your specific needs are. The confessions in this book are scriptures personalized for the speaker. You are basically speaking God's word over yourself. As you read them, do not just read them. Speak aloud with faith, authority, and power. You are partnering with God to activate His perfect will for your life. Let today be the day that you accept that God has more for you. Make the confessions a staple in your prayer life and watch how you overcome negativity and begin to receive God's abundance.

~CONFESSIONS FOR OVERCOMING~

- I will not be overcome by evil, I will overcome evil with good. (Romans 12:21)

- I know that Jesus told me that in Him I have peace, but to expect tribulation. Take heart; He already overcame the world. (John 16:33)

- I will not entertain a person who stirs up division, after warning them once or twice, I will have nothing more to do with him. (Titus 3:10)

- I will not be deceived: "Bad company ruins good morals."(1 Corinthians 15:33)

- I destroy every argument and every negative opinion that opposes the word of God, even the ones in my mind, and I take every thought that doesn't line up with the Word of God. (2 Corinthians 10:5)

- I can do all things through him who strengthens me. (Philippians 4:13)

- I will give thanks in all circumstances; for this is the will of God in Christ Jesus for me no matter the circumstances. (1 Thessalonians 5:18)

- I want to be the good person who shows up daily out of the good treasure of my heart, who produces good, and not the evil person out of his evil treasure and produces evil, for out of the abundance of the heart his mouth speaks. (Luke 6:45)

~CHAPTER 13~

REPOSITION

D oing the same thing over and over expecting a different result is called insanity. You are obviously not insane because I can only assume you are reading this because you are looking to change position. Life brings many changes and in order to prevail we have to learn the art of adjusting. There is an art to navigating that you must learn after birthing your purpose. There are many levels required to get to more that God has for you. There is a level of courage that is required to confront yourself. A level of strength to fight failure, a level of facing your past, a level of overcoming the fact that life isn't fair and a level of divine correction, ultimately guiding you to change positions. In order to reposition yourself there has to be a change in your position in three key areas of ourselves-mind, body and spirit. There has to be an alignment with the will of God in the mind, body and spirit. There has to be an agreement that has to take place in the spirit and the natural for continued birthing to occur. You have to have faith in God to see more for yourself.

It is never easy and rarely done without pain, in order to make the necessary changes for growth. It requires a shift~Nadia Olivia

PRINCIPLE #3: REPOSITION YOURSELF- MIND, BODY & SPIRIT

Lay Your Foundation

Repositioning requires a strong level of faith. *"Now faith is the substance of things hoped for and not seen." ~Hebrews 11:1.* You must have faith and believe that the Lord orders your steps in order to expand your vision to see the unseen. In everything you do you must have faith in God to see it through even when you don't see it. As an entrepreneur, faith has been a necessity and not a choice. In order to move into your more, you must be grounded in faith because the truth is you have to move blindly. Solely trusting and standing on God's Word. To start, all you need is faith as small as a mustard seed and as you grow so will your faith. So again, count it joy in the midst of trials because your faith is building.

"Faith is like a film, it takes time to develop." ~ Dr. Rev. Lashley.

Expand Your Vision

Expand means to make large things. So it's time for you to increase the vision. Write down everything that God has shown you for your life. Habakkuk 2:2, states, *"And the Lord answered me: "Write the vision and make it plain on tablets, so he may run who reads it."* Even those things that you are afraid of because it seems too big for you to even conceive. You must receive God's vision for your life, by believing with childlike faith. Even when you can't see, you must believe it with your whole heart. I remember before my business was up and running I dressed like a CEO and I carried myself as one. I showed up everyday like I wanted to be addressed. Allow yourself to expand the vision by seeing, speaking and acting like you have 20/20 vision. Don't limit yourself. No more dimming your light. Nothing is too small for God.

Build, Battle & Pray

Now that the cute stuff is out of the way it comes down to the hard work. Faith without work is dead. In order to position yourself for more you have to be ready to get dirty. Sometimes it requires you to use three hands. Yes, I said three! I know we don't have three hands but in other words I mean juggle. Some days are going to require you to build, battle and pray. As my mother says, "it's time to tie up your waist and pull up your bootstraps." Focus on what God has shown you and get to work. This actually requires moving yourself out of the way as well. Nehemiah teaches us that we have to learn to battle and build at the same time. Which means we need discipline to actually complete the process. Nehemiah 6:3 says, *"I am doing a great work and I cannot come down."* Some would say this is selfish but I have realized it's not. How can you be selfish when you are doing the work of the Lord. When God tells you to do something, it's wise to be obedient and do it. Sounds easy but it requires a great strength to not allow people and things that seem important to take importance. Distractions of all sorts will come, even in those we love. Distractions will come but we must stay focused and remember our greatness is at stake.

Walk in Authority

Not only do our thoughts and actions have to change but so does our posture. This might even require a new wardrobe. Take off your graves clothes, take off the cloak of heaviness. Put on the garment of praise and a coat of humility. Stand up straight, wash your face and act like your daddy is the owner of a cattle on a thousand hills. You have been given Kingdom Authority by your Father in heaven. Jesus Christ died so we can have authority in Him. And Jesus came and spoke to them, saying, *"All authority has been given to Me in heaven and on earth"* Matthew 28:18. The enemy had been defeated! Victory was secured on the cross Beloved, in order to walk in power, you need to understand authority. It's the radical, empowering, safe-keeping, life-changing power that Jesus purchased for you on the cross. That means YOU have authority to do absolutely everything God has called you to do in this life.

When you are ready to walk in Kingdom Authority, here are a few of the things that will be accessible to you:

1. *Radical Faith- It becomes easy to have radical faith. You will be able to pray with power and see radical answers. Your heart and spirit will suddenly be able to reach out and grasp God's promises that you weren't able to comprehend or receive for yourself before.*

2. *Divine Alignment- You will know how to align yourself underneath Godly spiritual covering and protection, so you will be safe in spiritual warfare.*

3. *Kingdom Knowledge- You will know exactly what to do to release the Kingdom of God everywhere you go.*

4. *Divine Peace- You will have an unexplainable peace that can only be given by the Holy Spirit.*

5. *Shift the Atmosphere-You can change the atmosphere and see people's hearts change and you will receive favor in your life.*

6. *Speak with Authority-You will be able to call forth the hidden things God has for your life- opportunities, relationships, and new ideas-and see them manifest.*

7. ***Kingdom Assignment****-You will understand how Jesus' miracle ministry worked, and you can begin to walk in the same power when you line up with His authority.*

8. ***Discernment****-You will be able to spot the traps of the enemy a mile away.*

   You will know exactly how to avoid drama and distractions with which the enemy would love to ensnare you.

9. ***Holy Boldness****-You will have holy boldness to release the Kingdom of God through you so that you can impart the grace on your life to other people.*

So, are you ready to reposition your mind, body and spirit so you can walk in Kingdom Authority?

~CONFESSIONS FOR REPOSITIONING~

- I believe the Lord is my shepherd, I shall not want. He makes me lie down in green pastures. He leads me beside the still waters. He restores my soul. He leads me in paths of righteousness for his name's sake. Even though I walk through the valley of the shadow of death, I will fear no evil, for you are with me; your rod and your staff, they comfort me. You prepare a table before me in the presence of my enemies; you anoint my head with oil; my cup overflows... (Psalm 23)

- I will not barely listen to the word, and deceive myself. I will do what it says. (James 1:22)

- I will be very careful about how I live, not as unwise but as wise, making the most of every opportunity, because the days are evil. Now, I will not be foolish, but I will be able to understand what the Lord's will is. (Ephesians 5:15-17)

- I will walk in righteous integrity- I am blessed and I will be known by my actions, and my conduct is pure and upright. (Proverbs 20:7,11)

- I will wait for the Lord and He will renew their strength; I will mount up with wings like eagles; I will run and not be weary; I will walk and not faint. (Isaiah 40:31)

- I am blessed and I remain steadfast under trial, I will have stood the test I will receive the crown of life, which God has promised to those who love him. (James 1:12)

- I will not grow weary of doing good, for in due season we will reap, if I do not give up. (Galatians 6:9)

- I rejoice in hope, patient in tribulation, and I am constant in prayer. (Romans 12:12)

CHAPTER 14

EXPERIENCE

*"Lord, You keep covenant and mercy with those who
love You and keep Your commandments."*
~John 3:16-17

PRINCIPLE #4: EXPERIENCE GOD'S BEST FOR YOUR LIFE

~OBEY~

Obedience is better than sacrifice. All who obey His commandments will grow in wisdom. Obedience provides a way for God to move. Agreeing to obey His word makes a way for Him to move in and have His way. Let Go and Let God.

~TRUST~

Believe that God will do the impossible for your life. Trust in the Lord with all your heart. Trust and wait for what is unseen.

Faith is about trusting God when you have unanswered questions. Trust only in God because He is a way maker. God has a plan. Trust it, live it and enjoy it. Have no expectations for man only God.

~SERVE~

Serve God with a joyful heart. You have nothing to prove. Serve God with integrity. When we serve others we serve God. Serving takes your eyes off of you and puts it on others, it brings a fresh perspective. To be a true servant mens to live a life of humility.

~LEAD~

Lead people unto God and not unto yourself. John Maxwell said, "leaders don't create followers, they create more leaders. Listen intently, have understanding, act intentionally, build relationships, empower others, provide solutions, stay humble, be authentic and keep a steady course.

I know it seems like a lot but when you make up your mind to live for God and make a commitment to His standards, it becomes a way of living. Practicing these steps daily will allow you to live in the experience of God. I could say it's easy but I would be lying but it sure is worth it. In order to move into the fullness of God you must understand Him and His gifts that are given freely but we don't use them as we should. Once you have said "yes" to His will they are yours forever. He gives us grace, mercy and favor. Grace is free and unmerited blessings of God. Mercy is God not punishing us as we deserve. Favor is God's supernatural influence in our lives. It's time to position yourself to birth the purpose God has intended for your life. Discover the treasure within.

~CONFESSIONS FOR AN EXPERIENCE~

- I am a conqueror in all things because of Him who loves us. (Romans 8:37)

- I was made for more and so I will be and do more in every area of my life.

- I declare in the name of Jesus that I will arise and allow myself to experience the glory of God in my life and become the mighty woman of God I was called to be.

- I am God's workmanship, created in Christ Jesus for good works, which God prepared beforehand. (Ephesians 2:10)

- The Lord will anoint me to fulfill His calling for my life and I will be His mouthpiece.

- I will remind myself that the joy of the Lord is my strength. (Nehemiah 8:10)

- I will stand up for those who cannot stand on their own: I will be a voice for the voiceless. (Proverbs 31:8-9)

- I will bear fruit because the Lord chose and appointed me. (John 15:16)

You are a Treasured Daughter of the Most High God.

Never forget that!

You are worthy, You are beautiful and You are loved!

It's time to get in position!

It's time to come out... Rise up and recieve what is yours!

Prayer is your greatest weapon, Use it!

Go Be GREAT!

With Love,
Nadia